1988

The Specialty Store and its Advertising

How to Plan it/How to Create it/How to Improve it

Judy Young Ocko & M.L. Rosenblum

Published by the Sales Promotion Division, National Retail Merchants Association, New York, N. Y.

FOREWORD

The National Retail Merchants Association represents not only the largest department stores and general merchandise chains in the world, but also tens of thousands of stores of all sizes including various types of specialty stores. NRMA has published a number of books in particular areas of sales promotion. However, we felt that particular guidance for the smaller retailer was insufficient, particularly for the specialty store operation.

Therefore, we turned to two outstanding collaborators and practitioners in retail advertising, whom we were confident would be best qualified to write an authoritative, practical and readable book to be entitled "THE SPECIALTY STORE AND ITS ADVERTISING" — Judy Young Ocko and M. L. Rosenblum.

The result is a book, which, if digested and given frequent reference, will insure better planning and more professional execution of advertising in all media by specialty store retailers. Indeed, this volume should be recommended reading for all concerned with supervising and preparing any retail advertising.

Joseph R. Rowen
Vice President, Sales Promotion Division
National Retail Merchants Association

TABLE OF CONTENTS

INTRODUCTION

Cover design and illustrated pages by Bernard Goldberg

INTRODUCTION

You've probably been told that, whether you're a giant Macy's or a little mama-and-papa operation, the principles of good advertising are the same. All you have to do is adapt those principles.

In theory, this is true. However, in working with our specialty store clients, we both discovered that they have problems which are unique to them, problems that do not exist for big stores. Where do you find the answers to these problems? As far as we know, no single book deals with the specialty store and its advertising in depth. Which is why this was written. It covers every phase of advertising, from working up a schedule before you start the ad to measuring the results after your ad has run. And everything in between. Always from your special point of view.

So if you're smaller than a department store but bigger than a pushcart, this book is meant for you. We hope you find it interesting. We're sure you'll find it profitable.

Judy Young Ocko
Morris L. Rosenblum
April 1976

CHAPTER 1.

WHO IS WHO?

Before you even begin to consider your advertising, there are some questions you must ask yourself. And answer honestly.

Who are you?

Who are your customers?

Who do they think you are?

The answers to these questions determine everything, from the merchandise you advertise, to where you advertise it, to the kind of advertising you do. Until you establish these basics, you're at sea... without a compass, even without an engine, oar, or sail.

Who are you?

You have to know this so you'll know where you're going. If you're a dowdy dowager of a store, with customers to match... to give an obvious example... you won't put all your swimsuit promotion dollars behind The String.

That's hyperbole. But consider this. Deep inside a lot of specialty store owners is the desire to be a sort of Bergdorf Goodman, the classy store in the area, with advertising that rivals Bloomingdale's or Neiman Marcus.

That's fine IF there are enough women in your market area who can afford those little $130 cottons and $300 Ultrasuedes. If you're in Grosse Point, Mich., or Short Hills, N.J. .... sure. But if 90% of the people who read your ads think they're splurging when they pay $25 for a pair of pants ... watch out. Or if a branch of a big store with a good fashion reputation is attracting all the customers with money in their Vuitton wallets ... can you afford the investment, in stock and advertising, to lure them into your store?

This does not mean you can't trade up.

This does not mean you can't be a good store, with good fashion and good advertising that brings in the well-heeled women as well as the masses.

What it does do is show you where your emphasis should be.

By the same criteria, if you're a promotional store that people primarily shop for the specials you advertise, admit that to yourself. Even if you don't like it. Once you acknowledge that, you can try to change it. If that's what you want to do.

Where do you get this kind of information about your market area?

Your newspaper and local radio station can supply you with stacks of demographics on the area: income and disposable income, education, age ranges, size of family, cost of home, how many cars, etc.

If you have charge accounts and clear them with a credit bureau, they can help. Or your own bank.

Then you can see if, in sheer numbers, there are enough potential customers for the kind of store you'd like to be. And the kind of ads you'd like to run.

Who is your customer?

Is she the local swinging single or a middle-aged matron?

Is she a junior with far-out taste or a half-sized mama... or grandma?

Is she a working woman or a harried mother with only a few minutes to shop... or a lady of too much leisure who fills her hours by shopping?

Does she wait to use the family car to get to you... or does she have a car of her own?

Does she buy her special occasion fashions at your store... and everything else at the local discountery?

Are you near a college town?

2

Are you jammed with high school kids on Saturdays?

Are you dressing women whose mothers and grandmothers shopped at your store?

You can get most of the answers to these questions, and others like them, by looking at your customers, and looking over what's selling. It's as simple as that.

Then you can develop what's known as a profile of your average customer. Just a fancy way of saying: who shops at your store.

Sometimes you get unexpected results. One of our clients was buying the kind of merchandise and doing the kind of advertising he thought would appeal to smart women from 25 to 35. He was selling it all right, but to women of 50 or over. He had never considered them his market. (He was old-fashioned enough to believe that every female over 40 had to be fat and frumpy.)

He asked us how he could reach the younger women. We did a little homework, then pointed out to him that, in his area, most women from 25 to 35 were tied down to a couple of kids, a mortgage, and a tight budget. They were not his customers. He could <u>not</u> reach them at his price lines. And that he should gladly accept the fact that a new breed of women had found their way to him . . . and was helping him make some very nice figures.

There are, of course, times when it's important to reach a group of customers you're not getting. This, however, is a long slow project, involving everything from the way your store looks to what it carries to your advertising.

Who does your customer think you are?

Unfortunately, what you'd like to be . . . and what you think you are . . . are not necessarily the same as what your customer thinks about you.

One of the major chains recently did a survey of customer attitudes. They were sure they had a reputation for quality. <u>They were surprised to discover that, for quality, they ranked #3 in their trading area!</u>

We know a men's discount store, where the owner (ashamed to admit he had a schlock operation) insisted that every ad talk about his fine suits and how the most elegant men in town shopped there. He drove his agency wild because the ads didn't pull well. They took the initiative and, for a week, asked each customer why he shopped there . . . and what he did for a living. The result? Except for a few students, a few middle-class bargain hunters, the bulk of the customers were in semi-skilled jobs. They couldn't care less about the quality pitch. All that mattered to them was that the prices were the lowest in town.

How can you determine your customers' attitude? <u>Y</u>ou can have an outside organization run a survey. Or you can do-it-yourself. Inexpensively. Prepare a questionnaire. Send it to your charge account customers. Tell them you want the information so you can serve them better. Or ask your sales people to hand them out. Or tack them on to a "contest" blank. Or use the phone.

What should you ask on the questionnaire? Among other things, where they have charge accounts. Where they shop most often (name at least 4 stores, including your own). Then ask them to rate you Excellent, Good, Fair, or Poor on fashion, quality, value, assortments, service, atmosphere.

Now that you know where you stand, you can start thinking about your advertising.

CHAPTER 2.

WHAT IS A GOOD AD?

A good ad is an ad that sells. It can sell merchandise, it can sell an idea, it can sell your store. But it always sells. Whether it's a screaming one-day sale or a chaste paragraph saluting the garden clubs. Whether it's a 10-second spot on radio or a minute on TV.

While we will primarily be talking about newspaper advertising in this chapter, the identical principles hold true for all media. Even your window signs. Good retail advertising is good retail advertising. Wherever it runs.

A good newspaper ad, first of all, stops the reader.

Research has shown that you have exactly 3 seconds in which to do this. Before she turns the page. Once she's turned the page, she won't go back. So you need a stopper. It can be a picture. It can be words. It can be a type style. It can even be a familiar or beloved logo. But it must have the kind of graphic drama that says .. hey, read me.

A good ad is newsy. Like your merchandise.

Have you ever watched a woman go through the paper? To her, the ads are news. The newspaper has been, traditionally, a sort of trade journal for women. This is where they learn about new products, new ways to look better, to improve the quality of life. For themselves and their families. Not just in the editorial columns, but in the ads as well.

A good ad gives all the facts necessary to make a buying decision.

Makes sense? You'd be surprised how many stores run sales that say 1/2 off ... but don't give prices. There are few things more infuriating to a customer than parking the kids with a neighbor, tanking up on expensive gas, fighting for a place in your parking lot ... then coming into your store to discover that the least expensive skirt in your sale is regularly $38, now $19. When all she can afford is ten bucks. Or, if she has a job, eating off her desk, killing herself to get to you ... only to find that while you advertised misses' sizes, in her size it only comes in orange. Which she loathes.

An ad must answer all the unspoken questions: what, how much, where. From can I afford it to what's it made of.

A good ad is convincing.

Today, when your customer must often make a choice between a scarf and a steak, it had better well be!

A good ad has an urge to action built into it.

So many ads just give the facts. Period. They should make the reader want to do something. Immediately.

A good ad sells your store, as well as the merchandise.

If they can buy the same Estee Lauder lipstick in 5 stores in town, why should they come to you? Sell your superiorities.

A good ad must be honest.

It must make what you're selling sound irresistible ... without exaggeration. Yes, it can be done. This is even more crucial these days when customers have turned into consumers. When they are more aware, more sophisticated ... and more suspicious than customers have ever been.

A good ad must be your ad, immediately recognizable as such.

If you can cover your logotype with your hand, and it's unmistakably your ad, then it passes this test.

A good ad must be timely and topical.

So your readers can relate to it. It must zero in on what they're thinking, what they're talking about, their whole way of life. The graphics must be of today. Simple, clean, dramatic. The language

6

must be of today. Conversational, not "ad-dy". This does not mean far-out slang. But it does mean good, current English. Not "garbed" or "bedecked" because in the last quarter of the 20th century, nobody is garbed or bedecked.

A good ad must be readable.

Not so gimmicked up that you can't relate copy and art. Not set in such small or strange type that it discourages readership.

Most of all, a good ad solves a specific problem.

A problem of how to present and sell merchandise. An image problem. A communications problem. Or all three.

How do you do this in a couple of small square inches?

With good copy, good design, good graphics, good typography. All based on solid merchandise information.

Few of us realize that an ad does NOT start at the typewriter or drawing board. It starts with the merchandise .. and the merchant. The better the in-put from the merchant, chances are the better the ad. The merchant is an important, but all too often neglected, member of the advertising team. He supplies the facts and the background from which good copy and good graphics develop. He knows why he bought the merchandise and for whom it was intended. Discover this and you're well on your way to improving your advertising.

However, be warned. Even the best ad in the world will not move goods that people don't want, or is over-priced, or of unsatisfactory quality.

We had this proven to us a couple of years ago. Macy's was trying to get a larger share of the rug and carpet business in the area and we did a series of ads for them. Each ad was dramatic, with persuasive, interesting copy. Each ad resulted in tremendous plus business. Except one.

Iran, where Persian rugs have been made for millenia, decided to catch up to the 20th century. They switched to power looms from

7

handweaving and to acrylic from wool. The first 100 of these new rugs were at Macy's.

Our ad was a good ad, by every standard. Including an interesting gimmick: we made a limited edition of the rugs by numbering each one. But the ad bombed. Why? The prices. You could buy hand-made-in-India wool rugs in the same traditional patterns for no more. Right at Macy's. So why buy machine-made acrylics?

A good ad can't move bad goods. However, if the merchandise is right and priced right, a good ad can move more goods than a poor ad. That's really all you can expect.

Can we also prove this? Yes.

A chain of small stores that was doing weak, old-fashioned advertising said they wanted to change it. Actually, they were reluctant to do so. The ads were pulling, more or less, and they didn't want to give up what success they had.

They were persuaded to try an experiment. For one week, run their usual advertising in the newspapers they used for half their stores, and run what we considered good ads in the other half. Then measure the results.

The same merchandise. The same chain of stores. The same newspaper space. Only the advertising was different.

Would you believe four times the pulling power for the good ads?

Would you believe that one item, which had dropped dead because they had presented it so ineffectively, practically caused a mob scene in the new ads?

That's the power ... and the glory ... of good advertising.

CHAPTER 3.

WHICH MEDIA ARE FOR YOU?

For almost all retailers, the newspaper remains the most important medium. Direct mail comes next, followed by radio, then TV.

Before we tell you the advantages and disadvantages of each, we'd like to issue a warning. If you have a limited budget, don't fragment it. Don't diversify your media, no matter how much you're tempted. If you spread your few dollars too thin, you'll make no impression at all.

It's far, far better to have 3 newspaper ads a week, than one ad and a handful of radio spots. You're only kidding yourself if you think you'll get plus business out of it. In the short run, you may move an item. But your total impact will be diluted, weak.

If you use the newspaper, use it consistently, then supplement it with other media. For special occasions. When you have the money.

This is true no matter which is your prime medium. There are successful stores that are never in the newspaper. They use radio exclusively. Or direct mail. They tend to appeal to very narrow audiences. Stores for out-size men. Or jeans. Or backgammon. Or tennis. The trick is intensive use of the medium. Whichever.

The newspaper

Its virtues are obvious... and subtle. Obviously, it's there. A reader can go back and look again. She can cut out your ad as a reminder. She has your name, address, phone number in print.

You can use a photo or a drawing in the newspaper, as realistic or impressionistic as you like. And the merchandise dictates.

You have the space in which to sell. Lots of persuasive irresistible words. You make the decision whether you want your art or your copy to dominate the ad.

9

No other medium lets you say so much. No other medium lets you play around quite so much with emphasis. The big, bigger, or even bigger price. Or headline or whatever.

Also, no other medium has so few technical restrictions. Like the lack of space in a booklet, the need for constant identification in broadcast.

These are the obvious advantages. You have other things going for you, too. The newspaper has long been a sort of women's trade journal. As we said, this is where she learns about new fashions, new products. How to be prettier, more fashionable, a better home-maker, a more effective shopper.

What are the disadvantages? You can get lost in a welter of ads. Reproduction and color, if you use it, can be bad. Compared, say, to direct mail.

Your newspaper may not reach all your customers. Especially if you have branch stores. You may be paying for waste circulation; readers who are geographically... or economically... not for you. A long talk with your newspaper rep will reveal this. Then you can decide how and where you'll use your advertising dollars.

There are other decisions you'll have to make. If you have 3 small ads on one day, should you scatter them? Build them up? Building them up... or sideways... makes a stronger impression. And you won't have someone's bunion pad ad sitting on top of you. Sometimes you may have merchandise that you can't make work together: a big shoe, a necklace, a long robe. (Pity the department store who tries to marry a garbage can and a mink hat!) Then consider separate ads... even if they're on the same page. Ditto if you use a vendor photograph for one item, and drawings for two others. If you have 2 strong sales and one regular priced item, separate the last. You might mislead the customer if you group them together.

What about special position or preferred position?

The amount of advertising you do, tradition, and the number of ads and news stories on a specific day dictate where you're going to land in the paper.

10

Most papers will honor your request to be on the society page, the sports section, facing the TV schedule. When they can. Some will charge you extra.

Almost all of them charge for what they call "preferred position", usually pages 2 and 3. The main advantage here, other than being up front in the paper, is that pages 2 and 3 usually have fewer ads on them, which gives you greater visibility.

There are two things you should always ask for. Ask for outside position; that means near the outside margin of the page. It gives you breathing space, white space you don't pay for. And ask for the right-hand page. When a newspaper is printed, the right-hand page is "struck" first. So you get what's known as a "first impression". Usually clearer, sharper printing.

What about color?

Effectively used, it can increase readership about 30%. The catch here is the effective use. Color as a background, color for the sake of color, and color that's off-color will do little for you.

Color should be used only when it enhances the merchandise. When it adds to your selling story. Then it's worth the money.

Many art directors are so bemused by the idea of color that they forget they're supposed to sell. We've seen big branches of flowering trees . . . with merchandise about the size of one blossom. So watch it.

Another hazard is this: your paper may have color only on certain pages. Ask where you're going to be before you commit yourself to color. If you don't, you may find your lacy bras on the back of the financial section.

Direct mail

It has one unique advantage. When your customer has your mailing piece in her hand, there is no competition. No news stories screaming for attention, nobody else's ads to district her.

If it's addressed to her, it's personal in a way no newspaper or broadcast ad can match.

11

It has a longer life than other media. It hangs around the house.

It lets you expose diverse and disparate merchandise at the same time. That garbage can and mink hat we mentioned could both be in the same booklet. You can literally have something for everybody within the pages of a booklet. Even lots of things they didn't know they wanted and might buy.

You can get magnificent reproduction and full color. If you're willing to spend the time and money on them. If this sounds like the answer to all your ad problems, consider the disadvantages.

Long lead time. You can't turn out direct mail as fast as you can turn out a newspaper ad. A booklet, for example, even a relatively slim one with just a few pages in color, takes 8 to 10 weeks from merchandise meeting to the customer's letter box. Do the arithmetic and you'll realize that your store must be ready with its merchandise plans for a November 15 Christmas catalogue . . . by Labor Day. Not easy.

Direct mail is expensive. To prepare, to print, to mail. Your buyers must be willing to commit themselves to enough merchandise to justify the cost. Also because it's expensive, you cram a catalogue. Which means little space to do any real selling. Picture, facts, price. If the item is communicable, sure. But most fashion is not.

Besides which, your mailing is as only as good as your list. We'll discuss that and more about direct mail in chapter 16.

Radio

Radio has immediacy and urgency built into it. This gives your message some of the same urgency.

It's the most flexible of media. In the sense that you can change your radio ad in a couple of hours, if necessary. While you should prepare radio on a regular 2-3 week schedule, you can turn on a dime. Sale snowed out? You can be on the air the next day extending it. The 10.95 pants selling out? You can substitute a sweater as fast as you can get to a phone. If your ad is live.

Radio goes into all homes, including those that don't get your newspaper. Or don't read it. Like many young people. They always seem to be tuned in.

You can pin-point your audience to an amazing degree on radio. Your station will have all kinds of demographics to show you. Who listens to what at which hour. Let them guide you.

Radio is inexpensive to produce. If it's read by the station announcer, all you need is a script. Written by you. If you're using other voices, it's merely a matter of taping.

Radio is an effective supplement to what you're doing in the newspapers. (If, as we said, it doesn't use up money and dilute your impact). The arithmetic is fascinating. If you expect a $1000 response from newspaper and $1000 from radio, and use both at the same time, you should get, not $2000, but $3000. In other words, $1+1=3$.

Radio has its drawbacks, of course, No picture, They can't see it. No recall. Once they forget your message or price or name, it's gone forever. Unless you catch the listener when you start, it's in one ear and out the other.

When should you use radio if you're primarily into newpaper advertising?

1. When you have a major event and want to reach everyone in your market area.

2. When you want to zero in on a limited group. Young people. Men in cars. Working women.

3. As a quick and thrifty way to test an item. Radio is rarely used for this. Yet, as we said, you can be on the air in a day, and get your results the next day. From a wider audience than traffic on your floor.

How can you use radio more effectively? See chapter 18.

Television

Today's glamor medium. Motion, words, pictures, sound. It has more dimensions than any other. The only place you can show merchandise in action. With a captive audience because you have both sight and sound working for you. In glorious full color.

The boss loves it. He's on TV, so he's suddenly in show biz.

Let him bust his buttons, but be sure to tell him he may bust the bank as well. TV can run into big money. To produce properly, to air properly. A 30-second spot once a week will do nothing at all for you.

There are ways of bringing the cost down. Which we discuss in chapter 19. So cost alone does not have to stop you. Just makes you pause.

TV takes special techniques, special skills. You may have to go outside the store to get TV done. To protect your investment.

It has many of the disadvantages of radio. It disappears from the screen when it's over. It limits your words, the amount of goods you can show.

But here again the arithmetic is interesting. Newspaper + radio + TV should bring a return that's 5 times as great as each of these media used alone. $1+1+1=5$. The new mathematics.

Shoppers, magazines, programs, billboards, etc.

If you're in a shopping center and that center produces a Shopper, should you be in it? If your competition is, yes. Strangely enough, the most effective ads are at either end of the spectrum: the bloody sale or the institutional. Regular merchandise seems to get lost between the steak sales and the banks soliciting business.

Magazines. If your area has one that reaches enough of your customers and potential customers to justify the expense, this may be worth considering. Provided it doesn't drain needed dollars from your other media. Provided you're willing to invest in several issues. A one-time shot is meaningless. Even if your pet vendor is picking up the tab. You should discuss this with management when you're making up your ad budget. And watch those early closing dates. Some magazines need your ad months in advance.

Programs, journals, and the like. The problem here is that once you're in one, every other organization comes to see you, hat in hand. It's easier to say "no" to one and all. On the other hand, your store may feel that, for public relations reasons, it should buy ads in every little charity's book. Just make sure that a separate budget is set up for these. That it doesn't come out of .. and diminish .. your regular ad budget. If you're committed to this sort of thing, save your energy. Prepare one simple dramatic ad that makes a simple dramatic statement about your store .. and use it over and over again.

Billboards. Only God can make a tree, so we'll be seeing fewer and fewer billboards in the years to come. If you're hard to find, they're great for directions. If you're opening a new store, they're almost mandatory at the location. Remember that a billboard is read at 55 miles per hour. That means 5 or 6 words at the most. If you can say enough in those 5 or 6 words to pay for the cost, hurrah for you!

CHAPTER 4.

BEFORE YOU START

The amount of advertising dollars wasted by specialty stores is enormous. According to the old bromide, about 50% of advertising is wasted. Which 50%? Nobody really knows.

However, one way to cut down on waste and give yourself a better than even chance that your advertising dollars will be productive is to start right. From scratch.

Make sure your advertising reflects your merchandising philosophy.

Get maximum impression from your advertising space.

Budget realistically and creatively.

In Chapter 1, we raised the question "Who do they think you are?" It's equally pertinent here. Ask yourself:

Do we run sale ads? How often?

Do we run classification assortment ads? How often?

Do we run fashion idea ads? How often?

Do we run item ads? How often?

Too many stores are purely opportunistic advertisers. They run what comes along when it seems likely to pull. If they looked at all their ads over a three-month period, they'd realize that they hadn't fulfilled any worthwhile objective. They had not told their audience who or what they really are.

So, whether you're in the newspaper every day or once a month, develop a merchandise advertising philosophy and plan. And make sure all your ads reflect it.

Before you start your ad budget

When a bunch of specialty shop owners get together, one of the favorite topics is advertising expense.

16

"My advertising cost is 7% ...""" ... Mine is 4% ... "

"Mine is 3% ... "

They all turn and listen to the 3% merchant the way the planets orbit around the sun. But be warned: in any review of advertising expenses, you'll find not only great variations of percentages to sales ... but also even greater variations in what, exactly, is charged to the ad budget.

Some stores only charge newspaper space and air time to their ad budgets.

Some are more realistic and include all space and production costs, both salary and non-salary.

Others call it a sales promotion budget and include all costs, from display to direct mail to donations.

So when you compare figures, get all the facts. That 3% could very well be misleading.

What should go into the ad budget? All sales promotion costs. Newspaper space, direct mail, TV, radio, magazine advertising, interior and window display, special events, fashion shows, public relations, salaries, production costs and supplies, special reserves, contributions.

That's the only way to set up a realistic budget. Without any surprises.

How much should you spend?

There's no magic number. It depends on your business judgement, historical factors, and a number of variables. Here are some:

Competition in your marketing area may make it mandatory for you to spend more.

If you're a new store, fighting for your share of market, you may have to budget more.

If you're a promotional specialty store, you may have to spend more. Promotions cost money.

17

A store in a high traffic area can usually budget less than one that has to "buy" its traffic.

When you develop a new classification of merchandise or open a new department, this calls for a bigger budget.

How to get maximum efficiency from your ad dollar

Most space salesmen will suggest continuity programs. An ad every week. Two TV spots a week. And so forth.

Newspapers and broadcast stations even offer continuity discounts. Which can be a great temptation.

But consider this. Is it worth saddling yourself with a fixed commitment for the sake of a few bucks? Such a commitment can be stifling, inflexible, and cost more in the long run. There are other contractual arrangements that you can make. That will save you time and money and allow you more flexibility. Ask about them before you sign.

Advertising continuity is desirable. But when your budget is limited, you'll end up with a continuous flow of small ads or a few radio or TV spots. Ineffective and non-productive.

Spreading your advertising dollars evenly over <u>every</u> week or every month doesn't make sense either. After all, your business doesn't flow evenly every day or even every month. Why should your ad dollars?

A larger proportion of your money should be spent when you have the best chance of getting the most ready-to-buy audience.

In other words, advertise when the fish are biting.

One store we know put most of its advertising into the Sunday papers. Yet Thursday through Saturday were the best business days. When asked why, the answer was . . . "Everybody's in the Sunday papers. We've been doing it for years".

Let's examine that logic. Or lack of.

"Everybody's in the Sunday papers". When all the stores advertise on Sunday, a market place is created. That's fine. But when most of your budget is blown on Sunday, without bringing returns in proportion, that's not so good. You had better take a look at how you're spending your ad dollars.

You can hold your competitive position in the Sunday papers. With a small, carefully merchandised, creative ad. Then spend more of your money another day. When it does you more good.

"We've been doing it for years". You know the old saw about experience .. that it's doing the wrong thing over and over again. Well, this is a perfect example. Your merchandise changes, marketing conditions change, customer shopping habits change .. but the big Sunday ad remains. Sheer inertia!

Note: there is nothing wrong in Sunday advertising per se. After careful analysis, you may decide that, in your market, Sunday is the best day for your big money. However, we repeat: only after careful analysis.

How to get maximum impression from your advertising space

Some years ago, the New York Times did a readers' survey. One question asked was "Which store runs the most advertising in the Times?".

The results were a shock, to every retail merchant, every ad executive in town. Ohrbach's!

Media figures showed Macy's first, followed by a host of other big stores. All of whom spent much much more in the Times than Ohrbach's.

Then why Ohrbach's? At that time, Ohrbach's did not advertise items on a regular basis. They were out of the paper for weeks on end. But, just before a major fashion season, or an important shopping period, they literally exploded in the papers. With a series of highly creative big ads. In a concentrated period of time. The readership was huge. The impression lasting.

The lesson to be learned from this skip-and-blast technique is obvious. But it must be tailored to your store.

Chances are you advertise three times a week. Many specialty stores do.

Your ads are about the same size as your competitors'. Maybe a little smaller or a little bigger. The net effect is gray. No drama, no excitement, no superiority over your competition, no memorability. No big impression like Ohrbach's.

The Big Impression... yes, you can do it within your present budget. How?

First, during the slowest periods of the year, <u>stay out</u> of the papers. Don't advertise, not even a modest holding pattern of ads. Don't let your competitors' ads worry you. They won't do much business anyway. We said earlier you should advertise when the fish are biting. So save these dollars for the Big Impression.

Then, make all your small ads smaller. An inch or two or even three taken from a small ad won't harm its visibility in the paper much. You'd be amazed how many dollars you can save this way over a period of time. For the Big Impression.

Finally, eliminate every marginal merchandise ad that isn't news, even if it means staying out of the paper that day. Your own ads and half-vendor-paid ads, too. It won't hurt your business in the long run. Save these dollars for the Big Impression.

Now... the Big Impression.

Pull together all the dollars you've saved and what's normally budgeted. Then spend it all impressively. On a big creative single idea ad or campaign. In a concentrated period of time. Do this for a week. Or once a month. Or even once a season.

Your customers will react... favorably. Your staff will glow... with pride. Your competition will reel... with envy.

How to prepare an ad budget

This is a complex subject. The bigger you are, the more complex. What follows is a simplification, a sort of basic guide for you to play variations on.

Most large department stores plan their advertising budgets twice a year. Then review it constantly: every month, every week.

Dollars allocated to store divisions depend on historical factors, business objectives, and merchandise emphasis for the season.

All expenses are considered and pre-determined. The amount to spend on storewide events, from sales and clearances to storewide campaigns. On divisional and department campaigns. On a contingency reserve.

The budget is broken down by media. How much for newspapers, magazines, broadcast, direct mail, even outdoor advertising.

All production costs... salary, non-salary and supplies... are estimated and included. Many stores also put aside part of the budget for the Sales Promotion Director. For institutionals, for special inter-departmental merchandise events, for the repeat of hot items.

The divisional senior executives then divide their part of the budget among their departments. They not only control how much the departments spend, but also how they follow the merchandise advertising philosophy that's been set up by the store at the 6-month meeting.

This is dollar budgeting. Large stores must use it because their operations are so complex. Specialty stores can use this system, too. But it's really too impersonal, too cumbersome and inflexible for a smaller store where a few people control the advertising.

It's far better... and more creative to budget by merchandise ideas. This is how it works.

Step 1: The working guide ... a tentative budget.
  a. Develop a budget for 3 months, based on historical events and a percentage of your sales volume plan.
  b. Decide on percentages for newspaper, radio, TV, direct mail, display, and any other sales promotion activities.
  c. Estimate all your production costs: salary and non-salary.
  d. Set aside a reasonable reserve for contingencies.

21

Step 2: Merchandise philosophy and objectives.

Determine your merchandise emphasis for the 3 month period by asking yourself the following questions. What are your merchandise superiorities? What will your customers want? Which classifications of goods should you emphasize? Which classifications of goods won't be advertised? Which price lines will you advertise? How much sale advertising will you run?

Now you have a tentative expense figure and a clear merchandise objective for the three months. So now you can develop the merchandise idea budgeting plan.

Step 3: Budgeting by merchandise ideas.

a. Lay out a three month calendar.

b. Review what's going on in the market with each department head and what orders were placed.

c. Find out which are the biggest <u>news</u> stories that have been bought to. What are the planned delivery dates? How much has been bought?

d. Enter these merchandise ideas on the calendar, the best date for an ad, the size of the ad, media in which it should run.

e. Go through the same process with each department head until the 3 month merchandise plan is complete.

f. Add your fixed sale and clearance events to the calendar.

g. At this point, the store head and the ad manager should review the plan. Does it fulfill the merchandise objectives? Does it come close to the tentative budget figure? If yes, that's fine. If it runs over, cross out the weakest stories. *Note:* If the merchandise stories are all great, maybe this is the time to go over the budget. You can make it up later, when the news is not so exciting.

h. Solidify the plan. Then hold a meeting with all department heads, the ad manager, display manager, and comptroller. Hand out copies of the plan, then make it clear that this is the 3 month plan, solid but flexible. If new ideas come along, you'll change it. If merchandise doesn't arrive when it was promised, you'll shift dates. Tell them to buy to it, because if what they buy is on the plan, you'll advertise it. And, the most important stories will be chosen for display, based on the schedule.

Will it work? Beautifully! Everyone is committed. Your buyers can buy, knowing that they'll get ads. The ad department can work ahead. They know what's coming. The display department, too. Best of all, it avoids last minute seat-of-the-pants merchandising of your ads. You'll know where you're going . . . and why.

CHAPTER 5.

HELP WANTED

If you're a large operation, you have an ad department, complete with a table of organization from creative head down to proof room messenger. With everyone doing a specific job.

If you're a tiny store, you may have an advertising person. One body. Copywriter, designer, production man, sometimes artist, too. All in one. This is probably the toughest spot to be in. Aside from the fact that no one person can do everything equally well, there is the problem of whom do you talk to. Yourself? It's not easy to generate ideas when there's nobody to kick them around with. Which is why consultants are so much in demand.

Most small stores, however, cannot find such a paragon. What, then are your options, and which will work best for you?

1. You can have a combined writer-designer-production man and buy art outside. This will work well .. if you can find the right person. You have an in-house staff, even if it's only a staff of one. Somebody who knows your store, its customers, is right there to make changes, to work with the newspapers, to call the radio station. Even to sit on buyers and get information and samples from them ... promptly.

2. This alternative costs a little more, but may work better. Have a whiz at design and free-lance your copy. Or a copy genius as your staff and free-lance the layouts. Paying the free-lancer by the piece, the day, or the hour. And, again, buying your art outside. This way you have your in-house staff of one, but also specialists in both copy and design.

3. If your ad person is a writer ... where the advertising starts ... you can contract with an agency to do both layouts and art.

4. You can have an agency do the whole job. We regard this as a

not too satisfactory arrangement in most cases. Why? An agency is outside. With an outside point of view. They can't possibly know you as well as someone working for the store and in the store. Besides, which, you are not their only concern. They have other clients. Maybe bigger ones who take more of their time and their top talent. The one time using an agency makes sense is when you do so little advertising that it's bad economics to hire an ad person.

5. Some newspapers will prepare ads for you. This is a last choice. For reasons that should be obvious.

Important: If you have a one-person ad department, as the store's volume and profits increase, add staff. Even if the number of ads you do is only slightly higher. As we said, one person can rarely do everything equally well. If you have a designer, add a writer. And vice versa. You'll get an instant and dramatic improvement in your advertising. Which, in turn, will give you better results for your ad dollars.

Where do you get advertising people?

Start by asking your newspaper and broadcast reps. They invariably know who's looking. And who's good. Ask them to spread the word that you have a job available. They can do it more gracefully than you can.

Get in touch with the nearest college and art school. Some fine writers and designers we know came straight out of school.

Call the large ad agency in your town or nearby town. They keep lists of applicants they have no jobs for.

It's not a good idea to raid your competition; they might raid right back. However, if you see ads either in your paper or the paper of an adjoining area that you like, you might make discreet inquiries.

Then, advertise. Not in the classified section, but a small display ad on top of or alongside your own advertising. A classified ad will only reach those who are actively job-hunting. A display ad will reach everybody.

128,343

25

Beginners or pros?

Actually, the ideal person to hire is neither. But one with a year or so experience. Enough to know what's going on, but not set in his or her ways.

Well, what if you can't find the ideal?

Beginners and pros alike have things in their favor. And against.

You can train a beginner your way. A beginner is eager to learn, has a freshness and excitement that can be very creative. A beginner will cost you less. However, you'll have to spend six months to a year training a beginner before you really get your money's worth. After you've done the training, chances are any good beginner will look for greener pastures and leave you.

On the other hand, if you have no time to train an ad person, you must get an experienced one. There is no alternative. No matter how many advertising courses would-be writers and designers have taken, you can't throw them into an actual working situation … and expect results. A pro will cost you more than a beginner. A pro, especially one who's worked for a long time at a single place, may not adapt quickly to your way of doing things. And beware the hack .. the person who just does the same thing over and over again … forever.

There are exceptions to what we've said. Beginners who will sit down and produce instantly. Pros who will improve your advertising overnight.

We hope you can find them.

Training writers and designers

There's only one way to train people. By putting them to work. Under supervision. By encouraging rather than discouraging.

It may take you less time and hassle to rewrite a tyro's piece of prose yourself or re-do a layout. Don't ever be tempted. Sit down and discuss it, the objectives of the ad, the approach, the problems. Then let the writer or designer do it over. And over. And over. Until it's right.

26

Otherwise, how can they learn?

We needn't add that you should be positive rather than negative. Find something ... anything .. in the copy or layout that you can praise. Start with that, before you tear up the rest. You'll get further faster.

Make sure the person you're training knows all the rules. Store policy, legal problems, newspaper restrictions, systems. This should be in writing. For ready reference until they become second nature.

As important as teaching them their jobs is to teach them about your store and its merchandise. Encourage them to talk to merchants (and encourage the merchants to talk to them). Encourage them to spend time out on the floor. Looking at customers .. and listening to them.

Who can work well in a vacuum? The more a writer or designer knows about the merchandise and the store, the better your ads will be. In fact, the best advertising people develop into pretty good merchants.

Too few stores realize this. They just sit a newcomer down at a typewriter or drawing board and say ... create.

If you're working with a novice, a visit to your newspaper and radio station will be a revelation. And worth the time it takes.

Mostly, don't expect miracles. Even an authenticated genius will take a while to adjust.

An uncomfortable postscript

You've hired a promising young thing ... and after a year, it's still all promise and no production. Do yourself and that person a favor. Admit you've made a msitake. Maybe the talent that attracted you will flower better somewhere else. Maybe in advertising, maybe in another field. But a year is enough time to invest.

embry's/ ultimate suede

embry's/hooper-bleyle

embry's/ DOWNTOWN. FAYETTE. TURFLAND

embry's/ sale

"Your logotype is an important graphic element". Here: a new logotype developed to do double duty. To link the store name quickly to a new fabric, famous name, address, or event. Left shows ad with the logo. Right shows 4 of the many ways logo can be used. Note that logo and message alongside it are in same type style. Size may vary, but not style.

"Designing a new logo is not easy". Sketches in developing a logo . . . to find more contemporary design, better relationship between name and chandelier, their symbol. Original at upper left, lower right logo chosen.

CHAPTER 6.

YOUR LOGOTYPE

A store logotype is like your signature. It's personal. It reflects you and your store. Good, bad, or indifferent, it's yours. It's probably been used for many years and a lot of expensive newspaper space has been spent on it. By now, it's a tradition . . . and quickly recognized.

That's why, when you feel it should be changed, make sure you're not changing it to suit your whim. Or anybody else's. And that includes the boss.

A logotype is particularly important to a specialty store. Big stores, who are in the papers every day with lots of ads, don't depend quite as much on their logos. The ads themselves are easily identified and serve as signatures. Which is not the case with a specialty store, with fewer and smaller ads. Here the logo provides identification, recognition, and personality.

How to use your logotype

Too many designers, in a burst of creativity, will often do a layout . . . then look for a spot to park the logotype. Where it will interfere least with their great design.

This search-then-drop-it-here method is just as bad as the always-in-the-top-right-hand-corner rule.

Your logotype is an important graphic element. As important as the art, the headline, the copy. It must be designed into the ad, not added to it. You must relate its position to the other graphic parts of the ad.

What's more, whether your logo is on top, in the middle, or at the bottom, it should always be displayed with pride.

How big should your logo be? Well, look at your newspapers. You'll notice that most store logotypes are about the same size.

Why? Tradition. Habit. And failure to analyze the competitive situation.

Instead of conforming to tradition, try using your logo not only with pride, but also with size. Scale it up and see how this gives you greater recognition. Instantly.

And recognition is what you're after, isn't it?

However, a smaller logo, surrounded by white space, can also give you tremendous visibility on the page.

(Advertising designers call this positive and negative emphasis. And they both work. Well.)

Some stores like to use their names in the headline as well, to reinforce recognition and for extra emphasis. Like "Bill Blass for Martha". Or "The forty dollar white blazer, a find at Jackson-Graves".

This is good advertising technique. But beware. The name should not be in the type style of the logo, but in the same type as the rest of the headline. Unless, of course, they're the same. Using a logo as part of a headline makes it hard to read. It looks amateurish, old-fashioned.

When should you change your logo?

There are at least 8 situations when change is necessary.

1. When you change your merchandising philosophy and your old logotype doesn't reflect this, change it.

2. When you change your store's architecture, inside or out, and your logo no longer looks like the store you are, change it.

3. When your competition makes your logo look old-fashioned.

4. When your competitors' logos all begin to look like yours.

5. When you expand into new markets and your logo begins to look provincial.

6. When you develop a new advertising format.

32

7. When you find your logo is not flexible enough or suitable for other media, like TV.

8. When you buy out another store or group of stores or change your store name.

These are the logical reasons for change. There may be other, more personal reasons. Yours or your bosses'. Just make sure, as we said, the reasons are sound. Not mere whim.

What should your new logo look like?

First, before you answer this question, ask yourself. What are we? What do we want to be? Who looks like us? As we said in Chapter 1, this kind of soul-searching is good for all your advertising. Your merchandising, too.

Get yourself a group of newspapers from different areas of the country. Look at store logos. Then choose those styles which seem to reflect your store. Don't copy them. Use them as inspiration. A starting point.

Warning: Don't mimic the logo of the store down the street or any competitor in your market area. The logo of a competitor who's packing them in is NOT the reason for his success. It's what's behind it.

Who should design the logo?

Designing a new logo is not easy. It just seems to be. The good ones look as though somebody just wrote them out or set them in type. Nothing could be further from fact.

A store we know wanted a new brush-stroke logo. They called in a great calligraphic artist. He sketched 50 different logos. The final logo was not any of them, but pieces and parts of the 50 sketches put together. Which took months.

Your catalyst is, of course, your art director, if you have one. He may design the logo himself. Or he may commission a graphic artist or calligrapher to work with him.

Embry's	Hytken's
Levy Bros	Wolf Wile's
Rodes	Hymson's
Bacons	Stewart's

Ben Snyder's
The Department Store

McAlpin's

"When your competitors' logos all begin to look like yours".
10 brush stroke logos chosen from 19 in the same newspaper
the same day! Some have interesting graphic personalities,
some don't. Some reflect character of the stores, some don't.

Whatever he does, expect it to take a lot of experimentation, plenty of time. And money. But it will be worth it.

Designing a logo is no job for a sign writer, or your artists. No matter how good these people are at their own specialties.

What to watch out for

Don't design your logo out of context. In the desire to be different, an artist may let his creativity run away with him. His solution may be interesting, but not practical for you or flexible enough for all sales promotion properties.

Make sure your logotype has as few graphic elements as possible. For example. You've seen logos with a "The" at the beginning and a "Company" at the end in smaller or different type faces. Don't make this mistake. It adds up to three graphic elements instead of one. Add these three elements to your headline, copy, and art, and your ad loses some of its graphic simplicity and clarity. What's more, the longer the name, the smaller your type must be. Incidentally, don't confuse your corporate name with your store name. To stock holders, it's Sears Roebuck & Company. On their stores, it's just Sears. L. Bamberger & Co. is Bamberger's. R. H. Macy and Co., Inc. is Macy's. All these names have been shortened. So they'll be simpler and bigger in advertising. Recognition again. Besides which, that's what customers call these stores! (If you must, for some reason, keep "The" and the "Company" in your logo, use them in the same type and size as the rest of your name.)

Watch out for outsize or very decorative initials. They may create graphic problems when your ads are designed.

Highly stylized typography may clash with the type you're using in your ads . . . or become quickly dated. The logo should work equally well in all your ads, whether they're small or large. For all classifications of goods.

It must be equally effective in the positive (black on a white background) and the negative (white on a dark ground).

THE *Fashion*

HERMER-ROSENFIELD

The Fashion

HERMER / ROSENFIELD

HERMER / ROSENFIELD

The Fashion

"When you develop a new advertising format . . . change your logo". Top logo was about 25 years old, needed refurbishing. The advertising format was changed, and the logo changed at the same time. Two versions were developed; for use in narrower and smaller ads, the other for wider and bigger ads.

It must look right in your color ads. In direct mail. On TV. On shopping bags. Gift wraps. And, with or without modification, on all your other properties. From the facade of your building to your trucks. On letterheads, store signs, even employee uniforms.

You can see why designing a logotype is no job for an amateur!

When is your new logo right?

When you're convinced that it reflects your store's personality . . . it's almost right. When it's different and better than your competition, it's almost right. When you like it, it's almost right. Then, when you've tried it out by preparing a series of sketches to show how it will look in your ads and all your other sales promotion properties . . . and it works, then it's really right.

How do you introduce a new logo?

A new logo can be incorporated into your newspaper ads in 2 to 3 weeks. Your TV ads almost as quickly. Direct mail a month or longer. Packaging and other properties, as long as a year. Should you wait for everything to be ready? No!

Go with as many as you can. Then schedule the others in a logical, business-like manner. For example, you may have enough gift boxes for another 6 months. Why throw them away?

There are two theories on introducing a new logo. One says: Do it gradually. Design your logo in stages so the transition doesn't startle readers.

The other says: Start all out. One day the old, the next the new.

The all-out method is better sales promotion practice.

Take advantage of the change. It's news. Don't apologize. Use the new logo with pride. Even run an ad, if you can swing it, telling your readers that the logotype is new . . . and what it now stands for is even newer and more exciting.

Can a specialty store have more than one logo?

Yes . . . and no.

Ideally, any store should have a single logo. In today's competitive market, it's hard enough to get advertising recognition with one logo, let alone multiples. Then, what do you do about a new Junior Shop, a Bridal Shop, a Beauty Salon, or a Boys' Shop in a men's store?

Do you develop a distinctive logo for these? Some stores do. Some don't.

Brooks Bros., a fine men's store in New York, wouldn't think of fragmenting the impact of its logo for its boys' shop. Yet Roots, another classic men's store in Summit, N. J., uses a Roots Boys Shop logo. Still another men's store decided to use its store logo in all advertising, including boys'. Here's how they reasoned. The illustrations obviously showed boys. The copy emphasized boys. The location line in the ad read "Boy's Shop" (or a special name that quickly identified the age group). Three solutions to the same problem. All workable.

A Bridal Shop or Beauty Salon can be handled the same way. Unless it's a major source of business. Then a special logo should be developed. Just make sure it's compatible with your regular store logo. Better yet, if you can, wait till you redesign your store logo, then do them both at once.

Junior business is still burgeoning. Especially when the pitch is for an age as well as a size. Many specialty stores find that a special Junior area, a totally different ambience, and separate advertising increase volume and profit.

We've noticed a trend to develop special logos for these Junior operations. Lou Rose of Santa Barbara, Cal., not only created a special type style for its logo, but also a special personality for its Junior ads.

Embry's of Lexington, Ky., uses a Junior logotype within their ads. (Their primary emphasis is on the store logo.)

Van Laws of Decatur, Ill., uses a specially designed logo.

The Smart Shop of Huntington, W. Va., has built a whole store within its store for Juniors. And, at the same time, developed a new logotype and a new ad format to go with it.

Conclusion? That, while the ideal for a specialty store is a single logo, a case can be made for another logo or two. But only if it's carefully considered and controlled.

It depends on the importance of the special area in relation to total business. If it's a volume-producer, then it's earned its own logo.

It depends on the amount of advertising space you'll take to promote the area. If you're going to have an ad only once or twice a month or so . . . forget it.

And naturally, it depends on how well you'll use the logo in your advertising.

CHAPTER 7.

HOW TO IMPROVE COPY

The best copywriters are not necessarily the best writers. They're the best thinkers. Sure, writing well is important. So important that we can take it for granted. If they can't put together a good simple interesting sentence, they should be doing something else.

However, a good retail ad is more than a fine piece of prose. It solves a specific merchandise problem. That's why thinking is so important. It's the writer who talks to merchants, who collects information, who has the background. It's the writer who establishes the point of view, the sell, who translates facts into customer language.

Obviously, this takes more than a way with the words. It takes an understanding of what makes good copy.

Customer benefits

Basically, this is the answer to the age-old questions "what are you doing for me?" Will this make me more fashionable, prettier, more comfortable? Will it make my life easier, be good for my family, make the neighbors envious, save me money? It can be as obvious as a bedspread that needs no ironing, as subtle as a new fragrance. But the benefit must be there. Preferably in the headline. If not, then certainly in the copy.

Benefit headlines for fashion are much trickier than benefit headlines for, say, a mattress. FASHION IN ITSELF IS A BENEFIT. Most writers don't realize this. When you have a piece of fashion copy, you are indirectly telling the reader "wear this and you'll look right". That's the benefit.

Unless you have a specific benefit like proportioned sizes, fit-solving problems (bikinis bought in parts), functional fashion (raincoat or padded bra), let the fashion news be your big benefit.

40

Did you ever hear of a woman buying a dress because it drip-dried? Of course not. She buys it because it looks new, it looks good on . . . and, incidentally . . . because it's easy-care.

The easy-care belongs in the copy, but the headline must be the fashion news.

No fashion news? Impossible! The merchandise would not have been bought if it didn't fill a fashion need. Even classics and staples are fashion news, of another sort.

Yet how often do you see headlines like "Polyester Pull-on Pants". The same old pants? Think a moment. Aren't these the pants that are the backbone of a wardrobe? There's the news.

Happily, there are certain words that say fashion. They change from season to season, but find the word of the moment and it makes its own news. Whether it's "denim", "faded", "natural", "big", or whatever.

Writing benefit headlines keeps you out of the two big headline traps. 1. The label heading. 2. The cutesy heading.

The label headline merely states what you have. Men's shirts. Misses' turtlenecks. Fleece robes. It just sits there on the page, without involving the reader, interesting the reader, or selling the reader. It's a total waste of space. The picture shows what you're selling.

If you're forced into a label heading by a format that dictates 2 or 3 words, use a subhead or lead-in to give the benefit. Unless you can give the news in those few words (you'd be surprised how often you can, if you make yourself think that way).

The cutesy headline can be so cute it's merely an ego trip for the writer. Again, this sells nothing. Like a swimsuit ad that said "A summer full of sun-days". How irrelevant can you get?

You approach

One of the wonders of our business is that we write for thousands, yet each person reading the ad feels that you're talking directly to her or him.

Capitalize on that by always talking "you". Be warm, friendly, and chatty instead of cold and impersonal. Use "you", either explicitly or implicitly, in your headline and your copy.

Take the headline: "This is the year to wear suede". It's a flat statement. Not a bad one, because it gives the fashion news authoritatively. But look what happens when you add "you".

This is your year to wear suede. Suddenly, the headline has become personal.

Is this your year to collect suede? Questions are always good. In fact, they're foolproof. They involve the reader, who goes on to read the copy in order to find the answer to the question.

Some of the best copy is conversational. Woman to woman, man to man, woman to man. It's an easy trick to master. Just make believe you're in a friend's living room, talking about the merchandise. You'll find that you're being personal, that you're exaggerating less . . . and convincing more.

Naturally, copy is better than conversation. It's deliberate rather than spontaneous. But if you can get a conversational beat into your copy, that's one way to improve it. Immediately.

Warning: When you're talking gifts or kids, watch your "you". It's the giver or the mama. Be consistent. Don't start a Mother's Day ad with "A robe to brighten her breakfast", then go on to "and you'll love the way it whisks through the wash". Don't mix your shes and your yous.

Be informative

Do you know anybody who wants a T-shirt in "assorted spring colors"? We buy pink or blue or green or whatever. Yet how often do you see it in ads . . . assorted colors, fashion colors. Meaningless.

If they are, indeed, assorted, at least say: pink, blue, green, and 7 other colors. Customers want these facts. They need them in order to shop.

Colors, sizes, fabric, price are essential. So are things like store hours, mail and phone information, whether you offer credit, whether there's a shipping charge, and your address.

You may get bored with giving this information. It may bug up your page. But without it, your ad is a letter addressed to Mr. Smith, with no address, city, state, or even zip code.

And who says you must always say "mail and phone orders accepted"? There are a score of other ways to say it. From... mail and phone? Of course! to... we love mail and phone. As usual, creativity pays off. Even in this area.

As long as you remember that there are no dull facts. Facts in themselves are fascinating. Why do you think so many people buy world almanacs? There are only dull ways of handling facts.

Be specific

If there were only one criterion for good copy, it would probably be this. Good copy is specific in its language, never general.

Let's take a simple example. Recipes are, of necessity, specific. Suppose a recipe called for ¼ tsp. spice. That's too general to do any good. How about ¼ tsp. pepper? That's better... but what kind of pepper? ¼ tsp. black pepper. Then you know. Or even better, ¼ tsp. Javanese black pepper.

Work through your own copy like that, getting more and more specific.

Don't say "a dress for every occasion". Because that tells the customer nothing. Except that she can wear it whenever she wants. She knows that. Instead, translate. A dress that will go from a.m. coffee to a nightcap for two. That's specific. That's vivid. That paints a word picture she can understand.

Don't use general descriptions. Like "luxurious cashmere". All cashmere is luxurious. Tell her what makes it luxurious... from the way it feels to the feeling it gives her when she wears it.

43

Stay away from words like "quality". Prove it. Labels like "better dresses". Why are they better? Phrases like "today's woman", "career girl", "women on the go". That's not how women think of themselves . . . as generalities. (Neither do men.)

Turn these tired phrases into specific language. Depending on what the women in your area are involved in. "Whether you're a chairperson or a den mother". "Young women who know where everything's at. Including fashion".

Be topical

The easiest way to get a reader into your ad . . . and keep her there . . . is talk about what she's interested in.

This is not the main burden of your ad. The merchandise is. But it moves your copy into today.

This kind of topical reference can be in any part of your copy.

In the headline: What do you wear when you meet the 5:02?

In the copy: If your backgammon is better than your backhand . . . Natural as a bowl of granola . . .

The use of an "in" word: For the liberated male.

It's a simple device. But it works. However, don't overdo it. Remember, this is a throwaway, a grace note to your basic copy.

Be upbeat

Advertising copy may be the most optimistic, cheerful prose in the world. Think about this for a moment. Copy is full of promises, it always talks the positive, always assumes that if you buy this, something nice will happen.

So why not be light-hearted? If your copy sounds as though you had fun writing it, the reader will have fun reading it.

Read your copy aloud. If it's easy to read and sounds natural, that's great.

If you stumble over it . . . because it's involved or polysyllabic, rewrite it.

44

Also watch out for the end that dies slowly. All too many ads end with sizes or ordering instructions or fibre content or a vendor's name. Add a few words of invitation. Come see it, come try it! Waiting for you, right now. You'll love it. Worth seeing. Plus all the variations on the theme.

Watch your language

Cliches are useless. Over the years, they've lost their impact. Like the picture that's been hanging on the wall so long that you no longer see it. Go over copy after it's written and replace every tired trite word or phrase.

Superlatives are dangerous. First of all, can you prove them? Secondly, if you say this is your biggest sale ... what do you do for an encore? Next week. If you say this is the prettiest shoe of the season ... what are you really saying about all the other shoes you carry?

Avoid typewriter patter. The little meaningless phrases ... they clutter up your prose, slow it down.

Watch your grammar and your spelling. If you don't catch the errors, nobody else will. Except several hundred literate customers who will laugh at you.

Keep your sentences simple. Ideally, one idea to a sentence. Ideally, always in the present active tense. I love blue. Not ... blue is loved by me. Why? Passive tense is slower, more involved, harder to read.

Keep clauses to a minimum. If the antecedents are absolutely clear, clauses are OK. Otherwise, turn clauses into sentences. Remember: these days sentences no longer require a subject, verb, and predicate. They can be only a single word. Naturally. Or a phrase.

Don't pile up qualitative adjectives. One that gives your opinion. If you say "beautiful scarves", beautiful is what you think about the scarf.

The other kind of adjective is descriptive: red, sheer, silky. You can't do without these.

45

Use verbs or nouns instead of adjectives. Or even adverbs. Instead of deep, luxurious fringe . . . deep in the luxury of fringe.

Try to find verbs with more action in them. Turn "see" into "discover". Turn "come in" into "zoom in".

Collect offbeat collective nouns. There are many ways of saying assortment or selection. A pride of fake furs. A glory of pendants. A bounty of blazers. Socks and more socks!

This is not just good copy. It's good writing as well.

Make every ad an institutional

Every ad, in its way, is an institutional. Because it tells the reader something about you, what kind of store you are.

Theoretically, every ad should state a superiority. You have the best, the most, the lowest price, the newest, the most fashionable . . . or it's only at your store.

You can't always say this. But you can imply it. In small ways. In your copy. Where do you find the new soot grays? At Blah & Blah, of course.

With wool prices soaring, Blah & Blah puts remarkable sale prices on all wool coats.

A look that's unmistakably Blah & Blah.

How can we do it? Easy . . . for Blah & Blah. We plan ahead.

If you can't afford institutionals, don't weep in your typewriter. Use your merchandise ads to sell your store. Your services, your ambience, your special advantages.

For example: charge accounts. Your charge customer is your most loyal audience. You want as many as you can get. Then mention your charge account in every ad. Even if it's only . . . charge it, of course. When you have space, really solicit new accounts. A sale or a hot item? Then . . . what better time to open a Blah & Blah account? Need a sign-off line? Then . . . open a Blah & Blah account. You'll be glad you did. Mention of charge accounts should be as mandatory as your logo.

You must never take it for granted that your readers know what you are and what you stand for.

There's a bridal shop we know that, like all bridal shops, does the most amazing things for its customers. Like sending someone to help the bride dress. This (and many of their other services) are never mentioned in their ads. Only flights of fancy about the gowns. We asked why. And were told . . . everybody knows about our services. Maybe everybody whose mother or grandmother were bridal-gowned by this store. But how about new customers, new fish? Even if everybody <u>did</u> know, repeating what you do for people is a good idea. It reinforces your image.

Which comes first: copy or layout?

The perfect ad team is writer, designer and merchant sitting down together to discuss an ad and establish a point of view. The writer then writes and, after that, the designer lays out the copy. Obviously, you can't do this on every ad. It takes too much time. But on major ads, on campaigns, it will more than pay for the time.

In most stores that produce good advertising, copy comes first . . . even when the ad treatment has been discussed with the art department. Except when there's a space crunch. Like 30 items on a page. Then copy must be written to an established measure.

When we say this, we often hear the alibi "we work on such a tight schedule that there isn't time to do copy first". Oh yeah? If the papers asked for a few extra days to produce the ads, they'd get it. It should be possible to find the extra time to write first.

Why? Because the words are important. They're the persuaders. The words do your selling. The writer does the thinking behind those words.

Writing copy first is not only good for the writer, but for the designer, too. Who will then not be working in a vacuum.

Of course, there must be flexibility and compromise. Whatever the system. If a headline or copy block is unworkable, the writer must be ready to change it. Let's not kid ourselves. There's no one way to tell a story.

47

What about formats? Here flexibility must be on the other side. If the format calls for a six word heading and a single block of copy . . . and you'll have a better ad with an 8 word heading and 2 short paragraphs, that should be discussed with the designer. And the change is made.

How long should copy be?

It should be long enough to tell the story and urge the customer into action. Not one word longer. Not one word shorter.

Sorry, there are no easy rules. But there are fashions. The current fashion is more words.

Good copy leads the reader from sentence to sentence. So don't get scared by long copy. If it's good. Witness the mile-long ads of Altman's in New York. Judging by their figures, those ads are read. Carefully.

However, if the copy is self-indulgent prose, it should be pruned.

Creative cribbing.

We all do it. Shakespeare stole plots. Artists have swipe files. Writers clip ads. There's nothing wrong with cribbing. Provided that you adapt the copy to your store, your customers. Never lift a piece of prose (even from a vendor . . . see chapter 13) without changing it. Because your store has a personality of its own. And your copy must reflect it.

We know some specialty shops whose ad men are really designers, but also do the writing. Naturally, they feel insecure about the writing. So they work their way through the New York Sunday Times. One day, their ads sound like Bloomingdale's, the next like Bonwit Teller, the next like Gimbels.

The result? Poor copy.

At least they picked stores hundreds of miles away to crib from. Even worse than cribbing literally is cribbing from your competition. It confuses the customer.

We know what happens. The boss comes in waving the paper and says . . . look at this Store X ad. They doubled their day. Let's do an ad like that. But he doesn't mean <u>like</u> it, he means the very same thing.

You'll just have to tell him you can't do the same ad because you're not Store X. You're Store Y with your own customers, your own point of view. What works for Store X won't work for you . . . especially after they've done it.

How about cribbing from yourself? Also known as picking up last year's ad. If the merchandise is the same, if the climate of buying is the same, if the price story is the same . . . all you have to do is freshen it to reflect today.

But be warned: all these "ifs" rarely hold true. So think twice before you blithely (and lazily) pick up an old ad. Literally.

A series of comprehensive layouts for a new style for The Smart Shop, Huntington, W. Va. The purpose: more effective, efficient use of space, stronger identification via the logotype, more consistent art style, and a copy style with longer, newsier headlines. All affordable, all reflecting store's personality.

p. 51. 3 examples of 2 col. ads, one with an editorial. Note use of 3 logos.

p. 52, 53. Large stopper ad for exciting fashion.

p 54. Assortment of a fashion category.

p. 55. Half figures, like sweaters, swimsuits.

p. 56. Omnibus ad for a variety of merchandise for Mother's Day, Easter, Christmas, etc.

p. 57. Omnibus; exciting fashion plus other merchandise ideas that go with it.

p. 58. 2 versions of sale ads. 1. Single fashion idea with price variations. 2. All-type clearance; listings by classifications.

Note: If store uses 5 pages of advertising a month, this style allows, for example, for 12 2-col. ads (36 items) plus 2 big ads.

Weekly use might be: 1st week, 4 2-col. ads (12 items). 2nd week, 2 2-col. ads (6 items) plus full page stopper. 3rd week, 4 2-col. ads (12 items). 4th week, 2 2-col. ads (6 items), plus full page stopper or 2 half-page sale ads. Lots of goods exposed and dramatic stoppers, too.

The Smart Shop

The Smart Shop

The Smart Shop

The Smart Shop

The Smart Shop

The Smart Shop

The Smart Shop

The Smart Shop

The Smart Shop

This headline
is set
in 24 point
Sans Serif

00.00

The Smart Shop

This headline
is set
in 24 point
Sans Serif

a.
b.
c.
d.

The Smart Shop

This headline
is set
in 24 point
Sans Serif

The Smart Shop

This headline
is set
in 24 point
Sans Serif bold

The Smart Shop

12 point Sans Serif
headline goes here

$8.98

The Smart Shop

18 point bold face
sanserif copy
goes here. Clpiqip
qllqiqilqlqlqiq
Ayqulllqlqllqiq
qlqlllqlqllq
qllqllllqlqlqi
qllqllllqlqlq

The Smart Shop

Our collection of beautiful shirtwaist dresses at pre-season prices

a. Sale 23.95

b. Sale 25.95

c. Sale 34.95

d. Sale $45

e. Sale $55

The Smart Shop

The Smart Shop's First Fall Fashion Clearance...Come Save

SAVE ⅓ ON DRESSES

LONG DRESSES

SHORT DRESSES

COSTUMES

PANT SUITS

PAJAMA SETS

FORMALS

SAVE ⅙ ON SPORTSWEAR

COORDINATES

SHIRTS

SLACKS

BLAZERS

SWEATERS

JUMPSUITS

SAVE ⅓ ON ACCESSORIES

JEWELRY

HANDBAGS

SCARVES AND BELTS

Save ⅓ on Dresses

Save ⅙ on Sportswear

Save ⅓ on Accessories

Sale starts tomorrow.
Doors open at 9:45 a.m.
Save ⅓ on dresses,
costumes, pantsuits,
pajama sets, formals.
Save ⅙ on coordinates,
shirts and more.
Save 25% on imported
cashmere sweaters.
Come early.
Come save.

CHAPTER 8.

HOW TO IMPROVE LAYOUTS

We all put so much emphasis on the way an ad looks that we often ignore its most important ingredient. The merchandise.

Yet an average-looking ad with good merchandise will outsell a great ad with dull merchandise.

We once ran a 2 column by 8 inch ad on a single shirtwaist dress. It was buried in the back of the second section of the New York Times. But the customers found it . . . and reacted. By mail, by phone, on the floor. It was exactly what the customer wanted. We knew that in advance. We had tested it on the selling floor. It checked out. It was reordered and then advertised. That's a fail-safe way to select merchandise for an ad. But there are others.

If it's a communicable item at a good price.
If it's a hot item at a regular price.
If it's a staple item at the right time.
If it's new and news.
If it's a sale, clearance, or special purchase . . . you have little choice; advertise it.
If it was advertised and sold well . . . keep on advertising it.

Selecting the merchandise.

The buyer wants to advertise what he's bought. The ad designer wants merchandise with graphic potential. The writer wants a news story. If all three were satisfied, you'd think that the ad would be a good one. But it doesn't work that way . . . every time.

For example:

The little black dress with a little black belt and no other details is an artist's dilemma.

Pearls aren't as graphic as an Indian lotus blossom necklace.

59

A white sheet is never as dramatic as a flowered one.

A "cord" suit could look striped.

A velvet carpet simply doesn't draw at all.

Does this mean that you shouldn't advertise the black dress, the pearls, the white sheet, the cord suit, the velvet carpet?

Or course not. If the customer wants it, advertise it. Recognizing the fact that real creativity is needed.

These are problems the designer should spot ... and solve.

The little black dress can be drawn to show off the silhouette. And beautifully accessorized.

The string of pearls can be a decorative drawing around the copy.

The white sheet should be surrounded by pretty atmosphere that will provide color contrast. Even if it's tones of gray and black and not color.

While we think that inserts are usually wrong and unnecessary, you may need one for the cord suit. A fabric swatch will explain itself.

Velvet carpet will always look like a gray blob in the newspaper. You can either show a corner of the room. Or use all type.

In all these examples, it's the writer's job to explain what the artist can't show. Like a radio commercial. And the buyer should be taught to choose merchandise that is newsy ... for the writer ... and graphic ... for the artist. If you take the time to teach him, he can learn to think of color contrast, silhouette, texture, or pattern. Any or all of these will help make a better ad.

How much merchandise in your ad?

Ideally, one piece of merchandise to an ad, regardless of the size of the ad. Unless it's an assortment ad or a mail and phone ad.

But, before every merchandise man and buyer faints, we admit the ideal does not happen too often. So we compromise.

Almost every buyer we've met has a formula for how many illustrations in how much space. It goes like this. If it takes 21 inches for an ad with one figure, then 31 inches can take two figures and 41 inches three. 41 inches is almost two full columns and that's a lot of space.

But are the 3 illustrations really necessary? Or is it based on the fact that most buyers buy 3 variations of a style?

You can't argue with the 3 variations of a style. They may need it to sell on the floor. But you can argue with the advertising formula. And should.

Formulas don't make for good ads. The buyer may be better off with one dramatic illustration that will stop the reader. And bring her in. Where she can see the other two styles.

Or, if there's lots of important copy, the 3 illustrations may end up being little more than large postage stamps. Suppose each illustration is of 3 separates. Do the arithmetic. 9 descriptions, 9 prices. Headline, copy, logo, etc. It won't work.

An ad is total space. If one large figure and 2 small ones will make a better ad, say so.

These are some of the arguments you can use when you have to cope with the buyer's formula. You won't win all. But you may win some!

Which brings us to what you do with the merchandise. The layout.

What is a layout?

It's an advertisement-to-be. It indicates what the ad will look like in print and should resemble it as closely as possible.

A layout is the first complete visualization of the ad.

It can be done from copy (the usual and preferable way in news-paper ads). Or it can be made before copy is written (always when the copy space is so limited it must be written to a specific word count).

It can be designed to include art that was done in advance. Or it can dictate the kind and amount of art.

Why do we make a layout?

First of all, to establish the size and shape of the ad as we want it to appear in the newspaper.

To clarify and interpret the objective of the ad.

To show the amount of copy and number of illustrations.

To determine the relationship and emphasis of graphic elements: the art, the logo, the headline, the copy.

To give artists, writers, and newspapers a definite form to follow or complete.

To give executives involved a chance to review, criticize, im-prove the layout. Before expensive and time-consuming final production begins.

How to make a layout

Most ad designers prefer to use semi-transparent tracing paper. This lets them adjust their graphic arrangements by putting one sheet on top of another. The opaque layout sheets given to most stores by their newspapers show column widths accurately. But they can't be over-layed, so the designer must start from scratch every time he tries a new idea.

A layout can be made with pencil, ink, brush, or a combination. As long as all the elements are clearly indicated and readable.

The layout should be precise. If you fake it, you're in for some nasty surprises. Like headlines that run over, art that doesn't fit . . . a whole bag of uglies.

62

The artwork should be indicated in its exact size and position.

The logotype should be shown exact size and in position.

The kind of type in headline, body copy, and prices should be carefully indicated and positioned.

Every element, from a manufacturer's logo to store hours to parking rates must be determined and drawn in the layout. Now. Not later, when the ad is on proof.

First, ask yourself these questions

1. What is the objective of the ad? Sale or non-sale? Clarifying the objective helps you clarify graphic emphasis.

2. How many illustrations? All equally important? This tells you whether you can feature one, or must design all the same size.

3. What will sell the idea best, copy or art? If it's an art idea, feature the art. If the story is more important, dramatize the copy.

4. How do I translate the material so my ad conforms to store format and personality?

Are you making these mistakes?

Are you putting too much into your ads? Too much copy and/or art will make your ads lose visibility in the paper.

Is everything in your ad too big? When everything is big, nothing is big. Contrast in size makes your ad more dramatic.

Are you selling too many ideas in one ad? It's tough to sell one idea, let alone several. Sell only one. It will pay off.

Is your ad too tricky? Too many angles, boxes, jagged shapes all excite the reader's eye. In the wrong way. They distract.

Is your ad dull? An interesting headline or an art focal point or both will make it come alive.

Do you fill your ads wall-to-wall? The best copy and the best art won't be seen if every corner is crammed. Buy some insurance with breathing space. The "white space" that you've always heard about.

And remember. A good ad doesn't feature everything. You should feature the picture or the price or the headline or the copy. Feature everything and you end up featuring nothing.

How NOT to get lost in the paper: the format

"A store style is an individual method of handling the appearance of the store's advertising, so at a glance, and even before the store's name is seen, it is apparent to the casual reader that the advertisement must be the product of that particular store and no other".
M.L. Rosenblum *"How to Design Effective Store Advertising"*, p. 107

A store style can be one of the greatest assets a store owns. What are its advantages? Individuality. Equity in building up easy recognition by the reader. And a pre-planned scheme for the creative team.

The more advertising a store uses, the easier it is to make the advertising style immediately recognizable. There's a constant series of impressions. On the other hand, the less advertising a store uses, the harder the ads have to work to create recognition.

Specialty stores, with limited ad budgets, must understand this and slave at creating and maintaining a consistent store style. There are five ingredients that, put together properly, make a store's advertising style distinctive.

1. Newspaper space. The way you use space, the consistency with which you use it, and the shape of the space all help in creating and maintaining a style.

2. Layout. The arrangement and disposition of black and white areas can create the individuality that's needed for a style.

3. Art. The consistent use of a basic art style, with some modifications and variations, is a vital ingredient in your ad style.

64

4. Typography. A minimum number of type faces and the repeated use of these same faces will give your ads recognition.

5. Logotype. Use your logo with "size and pride". The logotype will give instant recognition. But don't depend on this alone for an ad style.

These are the generalities. Sooner or later, however, these principles have to be put down on paper and developed into an advertising format.

This format comes out of the conclusions you've reached on all the elements that go into making an ad style. It becomes your bible. But it must meet certain criteria.

It should be flexible. For all kinds of merchandise and merchandising events.

It should be different and better. Better than your old haphazard, do-each-ad-as-it-comes-along style. And different from that of your competition.

It should be within your budget. If the space, art, type, and copy cost more than you can afford, forget it. It's not a workable format.

It must reflect the personality of your store. Whether it's a fashion ad, a sale ad, a clearance ad, or an institutional.

Agreed? Then start putting it on paper.

1. Review all your ads for the past few months. Note the variations in sizes and shapes. Pick the 2, 3, or 4 sizes that were used most often and look the most practical. If you run more than a page every week or so, see if you can change these sizes. Make the small ones smaller and the big ones bigger. You'll stay within your budget, and get a lot more impact.

2. Review your past ads for art. Line up your competitions' ads, too (you don't want to look like them). What art technique shows the merchandise best? What art techniques reproduce

best? Is your art too small? Too big? Too much art? Draw your conclusions, and then put them down on paper.

3. Review your past ads for the kind, size, and use of typography. What's available at the newspaper? What can you buy without breaking the bank? How can you use the type differently? Can you use shorter or longer headings? All display type or all body type with no headline? Are you using too much type? Too little? Is the type too small, too big? Too hard to read? Are your prices too big, too small? Again, draw your conclusions and put them on paper.

4. Review your past advertising... but this time in the newspaper. Not tear sheets, not paste-ups in the ad book. Will a border help you get identification quickly? What kind: a type border, a hand-drawn border? Will more space around your ad make your ad stand out from the crowd? Will a gray background give your ad the separation you want? Put your conclusions on paper.

5. Review your ads and your competitions' for logo and logo use. Is your logo contemporary? Does it look like your competitors'? Do you use it in the same size they do? Should it be at the bottom or top of the ad? Can it be used as part of a border? Draw your conclusions and set them down on paper.

Now take all your conclusions and put them together creatively. You've just developed your advertising format.

CHAPTER 9.

HOW TO IMPROVE ART
AND WHERE TO BUY IT

Every merchant is an art critic. He probably can't draw a straight line with a ruler, but he knows what he likes. And tells you. This is perfectly natural. For art in any form is personal. Whether it's a painting, a ceramic, or a commercial drawing for his store.

We say "commercial" drawing. The primary reason for a drawing in an ad is to sell something. A specific piece of merchandise, an idea, or an emotion. Art in an ad is a commercial tool.

Some ads require art. Some don't. You should not use art merely for the sake of having a picture in an ad. It costs money, takes time to prepare, and uses... swallows up... space.

Art is probably your largest advertising expense. Second only to the cost of your newspaper space. So if you're going to use art, use good art.

What is good art?

Good art is reproduceable.

The best drawing does you no good if your newspaper can't reproduce it or print it effectively. (There's a lot more about art and how it reproduces later in this chapter. So read on.)

Good art is affordable.

If it costs too much for you, it's not good art for you. But ... are you budgeting enough for art? This is something we've never been able to understand. A store will spend a lot of money for space. Then be niggardly when it budgets for art and production.

Be discriminating in your use of art. Use less. If you can't, use your best art in your most important ads. Your next best art (usually less expensive) in your secondary ads.

67

"The line drawing, one of the best techniques for good newspaper repro- duction". Shown here: how an exper- ienced artist can draw almost any intricate pattern in this technique.

Good art reflects your store's personality.

It should be recognizable as your art style. Immediately. It should be different from your competition's style.

A store that does a lot of advertising can use more than one art technique. But a specialty store cannot afford this kind of flexibility. Consumer recognition is more crucial. So use only one art style . . . with slight modifications.

Good art enhances the merchandise.

A literal representation of the merchandise, showing every stitch, seam, and button, may be good for a mail order catalogue. However, it may not be the best selling art technique for your store.

A fashion drawing is more effective. What's the difference between a drawing and a fashion drawing? It can be as subtle as a small change in a belt line or skirt length. It's a total impression; a good fashion drawing actually gives fashion information. It makes the reader want to look and feel . . . and identify . . . with the figure. And buy the illustrated item.

What should your art look like?

Your merchandise should be clear and sharp. The fashion news dramatized . . . by reasonable exaggeration.

The people in your illustrations should look well-groomed and contemporary. Not vacuous nonentities, but vaguely reminiscent of someone you've recently seen in the newspaper or on TV. Well-known personalities. Not portraits, of course, but reflecting their facial characteristics, their style, their charisma.

Figures should be drawn to look sleek and slightly taller than real people. But not 10 feet tall.

The poses should be natural. Never distorted to suit the layout. With figures always drawn in a position that best shows the fashion news.

Your fashion drawings should be accessorized . . . with extreme caution. Too many accessories distract the reader's attention from the merchandise.

69

Skip the atmosphere . . . the sailboat in the distance, the man in the background, the poodle, the hanging begonia. These can be useful at times, but they require superb draftsmanship and demand lots of space.

Note: While we've used fashion drawings as an example, some of the same principles apply to all kinds of artwork. With variations. We've said fashion figures do not need atmosphere. A home-furnishings or furniture drawing, on the other hand benefits from atmosphere. Not just any atmosphere, but glorious decorator touches. They set off the merchandise and make it glow.

The art of buying art

The country's full of retail commercial artists. By the thousands.

Most are specialists. Although a few rare ones can draw everything from fashion to cartoons.

Some want staff jobs. Some prefer to free-lance.

They're looking for you and you, in turn, are looking for them. The trouble is there's no central clearing house where you can find one another.

Staff artists are particularly hard to find. We once searched for a year until we found a good home furnishings artist. The specialty store, especially if you're far from a major city, has the most trouble. Artists prefer to work where the market place is bigger.

Where and how do you get an artist or artwork?

First some advice: Don't use your nephew or a friend's daughter to do your artwork. Even if they can copy Mona Lisa or draw a likeness of your grandchild. Pat them on the head and tell them to go to art school. Commercial artists are professionals; taught, trained, and experienced.

Get your artist from an art school or college.

While very few of these teach retail advertising art as such, graduates will have some knowledge of the mechanics of creating a piece of artwork.

They'll need time, training, and patience. Large stores can afford the luxury of developing young artists. And do. A specialty store, which needs only one or two artists, usually can't afford this. However, if you're lucky and find a young genius who can produce drawings that resemble the merchandise... or seems to have latent talent... grab. A good investment. Worth exploring.

Get your artist through large stores outside your area.

Big stores continue to look at portfolios, even when they're fully staffed... for the moment. They keep records of the artists they see. Call or write to the Ad Manager or the Art Director and tell him what you need. Many are happy to arrange a marriage. A good source.

Get your artist through advertising associations.

The Sales Promotion Division of the National Retail Merchants Association holds conferences and meetings a number of times each year. Go to them. Many pros in the business do. They know people in retail and they know the art market. Ask them. Then remind them by mail. They might be able to help you find the artist that you want.

And, of course, nearby schools may be able to recommend their students who have majored in commercial art or some other phase of advertising.

Let the word out that you're looking. It travels.

Get your artist from your competition (?).

That question mark is deliberate. Stealing people from competition is not good business practice. You competition can do the same to you. And all that happens is that the price goes up each time. The artist gains. You both lose.

However, if the artist is good, and leaves your competition for personal reasons, move right in. That's good business!

Get your art through art studios and art services.

We're talking about art, not staff artists. Free-lance art.

71

"Occasional use of a line drawing plus a flat wash works nicely". Here merchandise was best depicted by this technique in a decorative drawing. All art styles must permit flexibility.

There are a number of art studios or art services that will produce art for you. Single drawings or complete campaigns. Their fees are reasonable. They know reatiling and, even more important, retail time-tables.

You can find them in the phone books of most large cities. One in New York is Metro Associated Services. In Chicago, Ralph Heineman Inc. (The latter is atypical. They have many specialists and an art-by-mail service.)

Get your art from free-lance artists.

This market is big, often expensive.

The Art Directors' Club in New York and in many other cities, will give you names of free-lance artists or their representatives. The Illustrators Club in New York will do the same. Both have some retail artists as members. These artists are usually the top people in the business . . . and charge accordingly.

Any large city near you probably has free-lance specialists who work for the big stores. How do you find them? Your newspaper ad manager can talk to his counterpart in the city and get names for you.

Nearer home, there may be a free-lance artist or two, or more, in your own city. They probably work for all the stores. Not expensive, but probably also not able to develop different art styles. However, if they're good and can give you an art style of your own, you've lucked into a nice situation.

Art from manufacturers or your buying office.

All free or for nickels. But like everything else that's free, it leaves a lot to be desired. Some of the art will be excellent, some good, some dreadful. It will all lack your individual style. And you'll still need additional artwork.

Use it only for a special occasion, in an emergency, or when the art is so unusual that you can't produce it effectively yourself.

Use an advertising agency.

An agency can take the whole advertising production chore off your hands . . . including the art. This may be more expensive than doing it "in-house", but there are times when it's worth it.

As we said in Chapter 5, if you don't run many ads, an agency may cost you less than the continuous expense of a staff.

Agencies usually charge a fee for their services. Plus commission on everything they buy for you, from type to art to mechanicals.

If you plan to use an agency, just be sure it's retail-oriented, with a good staff and good art resources.

No luck? Then advertise.

Word of mouth is good. But when you need action in a hurry, tell the world. Use the newspapers in your local area or in New York, Chicago, Dallas, Los Angeles, etc. Advertise in the Fairchild publications, in Stores magazine, the NRMA publication.

Get in touch with placement agencies. If they can't supply candidates, they'll advertise for you.

Letters of applications and portfolios of samples should come pouring in.

Note about mats.

At one time lots of small stores used lots of mats. With newspapers switching to offset, these can no longer be used. If you do use them, use them just the way you use buying office art.

How to make your art look better in the paper

You have what you thought was a nice piece of artwork. Then you open your paper and see a gray blob. What a disappointment!

So you raise hell with the paper. It could be their fault. The presses could have been over-inked. There could have been a strike-through from the other side of the sheet. The velox could have been too heavy. Even humid weather might have affected the paper and the printing.

However, it's not always the fault of the paper. Quite often it's the artwork that causes the problem. It lacks good reproduction quality. Working together with the newspaper you can improve the blob and get something in the newspaper that looks like the original drawing.

How?

Let's look at a few drawing techniques and their degree of reproduction quality.

The line drawing.

One of the best techniques for good newspaper reproduction. A line drawing is done with a pen or a brush and India ink. Every detail of the art is drawn in black lines or black areas. Intermediate tones or textures are created by a series of lines or cross-hatching.

An experienced artist can draw almost any tone or texture or pattern with this technique.

The line drawing with mechanical tones.

This will reproduce as well as a line drawing.

The drawing technique is the same as for line, except that tones and textures are not drawn. They're applied mechanically by the artist or the newspaper.

When the artist does it, he applies a special pre-printed transparent film to his drawing. When the newspaper engraver does it, he applies the tone or texture on a photographic film of the artwork. This process is called Ben Day. There's a great variety of tones and textures for both of these methods.

This technique can give your art a mechanical look. However, a good experienced artist can produce fine and unusual drawings.

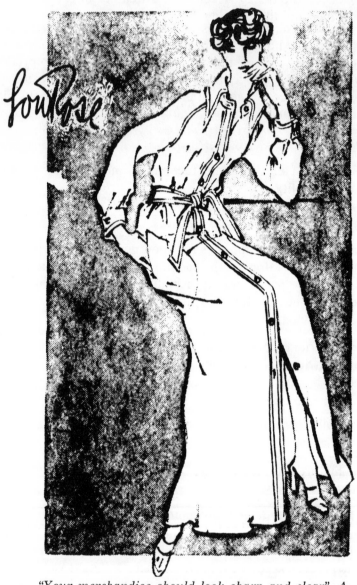

"Your merchandise should look sharp and clear". A white or light robe, such as this, looks lighter when a dark background is used. The contrast sharpens it. Mottled gray background, rather than a flat gray tone, adds character to the drawing.

The line and half tone.

A line drawing with tones and textures added in wash (water color) is called a line and wash drawing.

It's faster to do than a line drawing, and tones and textures of the merchandise are easily rendered.

When it's engraved, all the tones in the wash areas are translated photographically into dots. The darker the tones, the heavier and closer the dots. Conversely, the lighter the area, the lighter the dots. What happens is that the drawing becomes a complex line drawing.

This is the most difficult technique for the engraver to reproduce. He has trouble separating the line from the wash. So you can end up with a gray look where you wanted sharp blacks.

The engraver must "drop" all white areas shown on the drawing. If he doesn't, it will look dull.

If the wash tones are not specific, they tend to blob. Or print with hard edges.

If all the difficulties are averted, reproduction in the paper can be most satisfactory.

The all half-tone.

This is a drawing completely in wash. Effective for both merchandise and mood drawings. And quite simple to reproduce when the shape is regular (this is called a square half-tone). Most photographs are reproduced by this process.

It becomes a tougher reproduction problem when the engraver is asked to do more complicated things. The artist may ask (1) to silhouette the drawing (2) to drop all the white areas. The engraver can do both by hand, or mechanically or photographically. Whichever he does, it's expensive and takes a lot of time.

Unless the reproduction is handled with great care and skill, reproduction in the paper can be muddy (that gray blob!), with ragged edges or strange dropped out areas of dead white.

"What's the difference between a drawing and a fashion drawing?" Note "figure" look of the drawing, even though sweater is on a hanger. And how the little touch of a scarf gives it a fashion look.

What's the conclusion?

The better the engraving, the better your chances of ending up with good printing.

A line drawing gives you the best odds on good reproduction.

However, the occasional use of a line drawing plus a flat wash works nicely. Especially on merchandise like a camel's hair coat, a print dress, a fleecy gown, a sweater. All soft and textured or with elaborate prints or patterns.

The velox can make or break your drawing

What is a velox?

Velox is the name of a photographic paper. And, quite simply, a velox or velox print is a photograph of your drawing. It translates the drawing into "line".

The velox print is made, then pasted into position on your mechanical (see next chapter) with your other graphic elements. Ready for the next step in the reproduction process, the engraving of your ad.

If the velox is sharp and clear, chances are reproduction of your ad will be sharp and clear.

Why do we make a velox?

With the use of computer typography, more and more newspapers are requiring and preparing complete camera-ready ads.

The old method was to make an engraving of the art, set the type, then put it together in page form. This is cumbersome and uneconomical. It's still being used by many papers printed by letter-press, but will be phased out . . . gradually.

Newspapers are rapidly converting to offset printing. This requires camera-ready copy; mechanicals of the complete ad.

The velox of drawings is an integral part of such mechanicals.

Neiman-Marcus

"People in illustrations should look well groomed and contemporary." Line drawing with tones and textures in wash. Fashion news is dramatized, angle of handbag and stance add to the excitement of the figure.

Who makes the velox?

We'll be discussing that in detail in the next chapter.

What to look for in a velox print.

Check the size of the velox. Is it exactly what you ordered? Does it fit the layout? If it's too big or too small, have it remade. Or your other graphic elements won't look right.

Check the "color" of the velox. This is extremely important. Examine the velox through an engraver's magnifying glass.

Have the heavy lines gone too heavy? They usually go even heavier when printed in the paper.

Are the thin lines holding or have they broken down? They may break down even more in the paper.

Are the dots sharp and clear, or are they gray? A gray dot won't reproduce.

Are the dark tones too dark? They may very well go even darker in the paper.

Are the light tones too light? They may fade out completely.

Are the intermediate tones apparent?

Overexposure and underexposure are the two great faults to watch for in your velox. An overexposed velox tends to make everything too dark. An underexposed one is too light and loses all intermediate tones.

Check your velox minutely. These faults can ruin the effect you worked so hard to get in your original drawing.

Tip: You can add or subtract from a velox by retouching it. Black areas can be made solid with a pen or brush. White areas can be cleaned with white opaque paint. "Wild" or undesirable dots in a silhouette can also be eliminated with white opaque paint. But be very careful when you retouch your velox. Otherwise it will look hard and mechanical. Not what you want at all.

Bodoni 6-8-10-12-14-18-24-30-36-48-60-72

Bodoni Bold 6-8-10-12-14-18-24-30-36-48-60-72

Bodoni Campanile 10-12-14-18-24-30-36-48-60-72

Bodoni Italics 6-8-10-12-14-18-24-30-36-48-60-72

Century Schoolbook
6-8-10-12-14-18-24-30-36-48-60-72

Century Schoolbook Italics
6-8-10-12-14-18-24-30-36-48-60-72

Gothic 299 10-12-14-18-24-30-36-48-60-72

Poster Bodoni 10-12-14-18-24-30-36-48-60-72

Techno Bold 6-8-10-12-14-18-24-30-36-48-60-72

Techno Bold Condensed 8-10-12-14-18-24-30-36-48-60-72

Techno Extra Bold 6-8-10-12-14-18-24-30-36-48-60-72

Techno Extra Bold Condensed
8-10-12-14-18-24-30-36-48-60-72

Techno Medium 6-8-10-12-14-18-24-30-36-48-60-72

Techno Medium Condensed 8-10-12-14-18-24-30-36-48-60-72

"..find out what's available at your newspaper before you create a type style for your store ... Some have a good type assortment. Some adequate. Many are exceedingly limited". Left hand page: type available at Palm Beach Post and Palm Beach Times. Right hand: Shreveport Times and Shreveport Journal. Both use cold type, all give type sizes available.

Univers Medium Italic

Univers Medium

Univers Bold Italic

Univers Bold

Gothic No. 4

Gothic No. 1

News Gothic

Franklin Gothic

Bodoni Bold

Bodoni Bold Italic

Bodoni Extrabold

Bodoni Extrabold Italic

News No. 2

News Bold No. 2

Erbar Medium Condensed

Bodoni Extrabold Condensed

Century Textbook

Century Textbook Italic.

Century Textbook Bold

Cheltenham Bold

CHAPTER 10.

TYPE

Type is to read. That's its primary purpose. Every other consideration is secondary, even the design itself and personality.

Most specialty stores underestimate the importance of good typography. Their ads are filled with bad graphic habits and tired and false cliches.

Here are some of those cliches . . . and we quote:

"Make the type bigger".

Big is a relative term. While it's true that big type is easier to read, it's equally true that it can get so big the eye can't see it quickly. Or grasp the meaning.

Too much big type in an ad is like somebody shouting all the time. No emphasis. No modulation. After a while, you can't hear it.

If you feel you must have big type in your ads, use it sparingly. For drama and accent. Make sure it's surrounded by white space. That it's well-leaded (space between each line). That it's not set in too narrow a measure. Big type needs big space.

"Make the type smaller".

Too many stores believe that small type is elegant. Do they consider the corollary? That all customers who are interested in good merchandise have 20-20 vision! Actually, 50% of the U.S. population must wear corrective lenses of some sort.

Elegance in an ad results not from the size of type, but your choice of type face. The way it's designed in the ad, with a maximum use of white space around it. Type should be big enough to read easily. No bigger. No smaller.

"Nobody reads the type . . . cut it!"

Ha! Maybe this was true when we were a nation of illiterates. But not now. Readers want to know all about what you're selling. Especially today when customers have become consumers.

We repeat from Chapter 2: "How long should the copy (the type) be? Long enough to tell the story and urge the customer to action. Not one word longer, not one word shorter".

Your ad must be designed so there's enough space for the whole story. And not in mouse-size type either. Before you design it, ask yourself... which is more important, the story (the type) or the art? They can't be equally important. Not if you want an effective ad. The story more important? Give it the space it requires, the emphasis it deserves. Make the art smaller. Or skip it.

"You must have a picture or they won't know what it's about".

Type is a picture. A word picture. It stands on its own. The headline "Sale of Fashion Coats. 12 different styles. So you can find the coat you want. And save." is a vivid word picture. It lets the reader's imagination run loose. She visualizes a dozen different coats. How much better than the traditional approach. Showing a coat or two... "so she'll know this is a coat ad". What if she doesn't like the one or two coats you show? You've lost a sale.

All-type ads have been beautifully used for sales of assorted styles, clearances, services, institutionals, trunk showings, even fashion ads.

We once ran an all-type ad on Paris fashions. Basically, it was an invitation to a show of the new imports and our line-for-line copies. Our logic was the same as for the coat sale above. We felt that the names of the great Paris designers in an all-type ad provoked the imagination far more than one or two illustrations possibly could. The all-type ad worked. The show was jammed.

So don't use art in an ad. Not when type can do the job... at times an even better job.

"Make the prices bigger and blacker".

Bigger and/or blacker prices don't necessarily sell harder. It's not the size or the boldness of the prices that brings them in, but the item at the price. If you advertised new Cadillacs for $1000, you could whisper the price in small, light-face type, and the customers would come running.

A communicable item with its story in readable type and a reasonable size price will be seen and read.

In regular specialty store advertising, your prices should be set in the same size as the body text, occasionally one size larger or slightly bolder or underlined.

"Spread out the type. You've got some space left".

If you think you'll get greater readership by making every type statement a separate one, you're wrong. Yet we see this every day in specialty store ads. Consolidate the typographic elements in your ads. The fewer elements you have, the easier they are to see and read.

"I'm paying for the full width of the ad. Use it all".

Using type "wall-to-wall", the entire width of the ad, looks great in a layout. But when it's in the paper, alongside other ads, your ad gets lost.

Give your type the protection of white space to separate it from other ads and news matter.

"Don't use italic type. It's harder to read".

In readership tests, italic type has proven slightly more difficult to read than regular Roman type. However, a good graphic designer can make just about any type face, even italic, legible. Conversely, if it's not properly designed in the ad, even the most classic type face can be hard to read.

It's not the type face alone. It's the way it's used that gets you the readership you want.

Bamberger's used italic type in all its ads for almost 10 years. Neiman Marcus also used it for body type for a long time.

So use italic, or any other type that suits your advertising personality. Just be sure it's carefully and thoughtfully selected and designed.

"Put in store hours, addresses, free parking, charge accounts, delivery, phone numbers, etc., etc."

Special services are important to the customer. You should plan them, not shove them into a hole in the ad. They shouldn't detract from the major type story. It's not necessary to display every service in the ad. Unless it's a big ad with plenty of space. Or an institutional on services.

Many stores have tackled the problem and solved it. They set services in type that's slightly smaller than the main text. Then use it as a couple of base lines at the bottom of the ad. Smaller type, but readable.

What type faces for you?

There are thousands of type faces and families of type. A bewilderment of choices. Some are radically different, some are subtly different. The possibilities of type combinations are almost infinite. Like people, each type has its individual characteristics. Some type is fat, some thin, some tall, some short, some fancy, some plain.

Translated into typographer's language, they are called: light face, bold face, inline, classic, modern, serif, sans serif, condensed, expanded, and so on. These are generic terms. Each type face has a name of its own.

Like dresses or shoes, type also comes in sizes. The unit of measure for type is the point. There are 72 points to the inch. Typographers and ad designers divide type sizes into two categories: body type and display type. Body type is smaller, display type larger.

Body type runs from 6 point to 14 point. Display type from 18 to 72, and some type faces go up to 120 point. That's about 1-2/3 inches high! (The text of this book is 11 point type.)

In theory, there are thousands of type faces and many sizes to choose from. Actually, the number of type faces available to specialty stores is limited. That's because their ads are set by the newspaper, and you're limited to the type the newspaper owns.

So find out what's available at your newspaper before you create a type style for your store. Most papers give charts or books to their retail advertisers that show all their type faces and sizes. Some have a good type assortment. Some adequate. Many are exceedingly limited.

What can you do when you want a special type face for your advertising?

You can buy your typography from a typographic shop or printer. They may have a larger variety than your newspaper. Of course, this will cost you money. One specialty store we know decided they wanted a distinctive type face. They bought it from a typographic shop and made up the difference in cost by cutting the size of some of their ads slightly.

Or you can make a deal with your newspaper to buy the type for your exclusive use. This costs money, too, but it's a one-time expense. Since the advent of computer-set typography, this costs far less today than it did years ago. (See hot and cold type further on in this chapter.)

Or you can compromise. Use the body type your newspaper has. Then either buy a distinctive headline type from a typographer or use paste-up or transfer type. The paste-up or transfer method is not expensive. But it takes staff time to put together. One of the companies that produce transfer type is Chartpak. There are others. You can buy it at your art supply dealer. Reasonably.

Selecting type for your store

In Chapter 8 we discussed store advertising style. We said that one of the ingredients of a distinctive style is typography. We repeat... "A minimum number of type faces and the repeated use of these same type faces will give your ad recognition".

Here are the basic criteria in selecting type:

- Do you want your advertising to look traditional or contemporary? *Select the type face that reflects your personality.*

- Do you want to shout or whisper or sometimes do both? *Select a type family that's flexible.* One that includes light face, bold face, and a large number of type sizes.

- Do you want to be individual? *Select a type family the competition doesn't use.* Warning: Be different and better, but not tricky. A very unusual type face is fine for an occasional ad, a short headline, or even a single word. Using tricky type on an ad-to-ad basis leads to indigestion.

- Do you want people to read your ads easily? *Select a type family that reproduces well in your newspaper.* For example: Very thin lines, especially in small sizes tend to break down. Extra-condensed faces may clog up and be unreadable.

Indicating typography in your ads

How often have type proofs come back from your paper or typographer not looking the way you expected? Different type. Larger or smaller headline type. Longer or shorter copy blocks.

You could scream at the typographers. They may be at fault. But, before you do, check the layouts and your type instructions. You may be in the wrong.

This is a simple case of give and you shall receive. Type production men tell us that their biggest problem with most layouts is careless type indication. If type markings are sloppy or careless, they can be interpreted in many ways. Not necessarily the way you had in mind.

What happens when you fake or compress type in a headline? You get either smaller size type or a longer line. Large type should be traced from the type charts. Not guessed at.

What do you get with a haphazard indication of body type on the layout? Smaller or larger type than you expected. Or a longer or shorter copy block. Mark the width of the block and the number of lines on the layout. Count the number of characters in the typewritten copy. Match them to the number of characters in your type size for the space, according to your type chart. Then, and only then, will you know if the copy fits.

Tell the typographer the exact type face or faces you want set. Write this clearly on the margin of your layout or on your type-written copy. Don't let him figure it out for himself. You may not like his taste in type or how he interprets what you had in the back of your head.

Never, never write your copy on the layout. Even if it's only a clutch of words. Give your typographer a good clean typewritten manuscript. Always keep a duplicate for yourself. He'll have less trouble deciphering the immortal prose. You'll have a copy for checking proofs.

Hot type ... cold type

In the last few years there has been a radical change in the way type is set. It's called Phototypography. Even if you're not aware of this typographic revolution (and it is a revolution), it's bound to affect your advertising in some way.

Hot type, what is it?

As far back as any of us can remember, every line of type was created in one of three ways:

1. Foundry type; individual letters set by hand for each line of type.

2. Monotype; individual letters cast mechanically one at a time to form a line of type.

3. Linotype, Ludlow, Intertype; a slug for an entire line of type cast mechanically.

All these methods used molten metal to cast the type, the slug, or the line of type. Hence the name, "hot type".

Cold type, what is it?

Cold type is relatively new. Its official name is Phototypography. It uses a machine, most often a computer, activated by a punched paper tape. This produces almost instantaneous photographic typography.

Here's how it works.

- A mark-up man, following your layout and type instructions, indicates computer command codes on the margin of your copy sheet.

- A typist uses only these copy sheets from which to set type. Actually, it's like typing a letter. The typist follows the type marker's instructions. A special typewriter puts the copy and the computer command orders on a punched paper tape.

- This paper tape is put into a machine. Its type discs and lenses are activated at high speed. Then a flash of light captures each type character in precisely the proper position on photographic paper.

Some machines are relatively simple. Some have amazing capability. One machine photographs a letter of type at the astonishing speed of 1/250,000 of a second!

Cold type: its advantages, its disadvantages

Newspapers that did a good typographic job with hot type will continue to produce good typography with cold type. They have fine craftsmen, and take pride in the way their paper looks.

Newspapers that now produce marginal typography will not necessarily improve when they switch to cold type.

Why should a newspaper switch to cold type? Speed, lower cost, and greater flexibility. Some of these advantages could work for you. The faster they set type and the less their operating cost, the lower your line rate. Or at least, they can hold the line at its present rates longer.

Since computer typography has such type face flexibility, we all hoped that stores could get type faces for their exclusive use. In some areas, they can. In others it's a pipe-dream. When you ask, the answers you get from some newspapers are ... "our computers are at full type reel capacity"... "We can't switch type faces for one store"... "special type face reels for our computer are terribly expensive". All true. All based on the capability of the computer that the newspaper is using.

On the other hand, some newspapers own computers that make it possible to use a special type face for some advertisers.

Reels of special type faces cost from $50 to $200. This is a one-time charge to the store. And well worth it, if you can get it.

We said that a mark-up man and a typist were responsible for producing your Phototypography. All your type requests are interpreted and put into type by these two people. If they are good, and experienced, your type will be good. Even then, it will only be good if you're careful with the indications and information on your copy.

Hot type is set in a form. You can get as many proofs as you need. Cold type gives you only one proof... the original. You'll need duplicate copies for checking graphics and proofreading. These must be made on a copy machine. A minor inconvenience, but one you can live with.

Despite some disadvantages and inconveniences, many large stores, and some small ones, are buying computers. And setting their own typography. They have found the advantages of Photo-typography to be enormous.

Even stores in smaller cities are using computer-set type. Buying typography from type shops springing up all over the country.

Much smaller computers, far less expensive than the massive ones the newspapers own, are coming on the market. Their type face reels are modestly priced and their flexibility greater.

Phototypography is here to stay. Until something even better comes along.

CHAPTER 11.

PUTTING IT ALL TOGETHER

Once, on a consulting job at a specialty store, the boss was full of complaints. About the little things that went awry in many of his ads. They started out fine on the layout, but seemed to wind up wrong in the newspaper.

The artwork was crooked. The headline type appeared too big.

The store location line was in the wrong position. Or left out.

The key letters were often mixed up. The logotype was too small.

Even a price was occasionally wrong.

The solution? Much simpler than you think. We suggested that his advertising department prepare its own mechanicals, and promised him that most of these annoying and often serious problems would disappear.

They did.

The mechanical: what is it?

Newspapers call it camera-ready copy. Advertising people call it a mechanical. It's the final translation of your ad as it will appear in the newspaper.

Every graphic element of the ad has been pasted down in its exact size and position. Ready for the camera.

Your art, or the velox print of the art, your headline, your price or prices, your logotype, your copy, your key letters, your borders. Even the asterisks and registered trade-marks.

Sounds like a cross between paradise and the millenium, doesn't it? It is. No surprises.

However, be warned. If there's a mistake in the newspaper, it's

93

your mistake. Not the paper's. The final responsibility for the ad belongs to you and your ad department. There are no alibis.

But you do get a chance to look at the complete ad, in detail, in advance. Before it's released to the papers. And what you see is what you get.

The what-you-see-is-what-you-get is only one benefit of preparing your own mechanicals. There are others.

Some newspapers are actually giving rebates (or considering them) to retailers who submit camera-ready copy. Either a flat rate or a percentage per line or per inch of the advertising space.

Tip: If it's negotiable, ask for a percentage of the rate rather than a flat rebate. You'll do better if linage rates go up.

If your ads run in more than one paper, especially papers that are some distance from the main store, it's almost impossible to see proofs or make corrections easily. A duplicate of the mechanical solves that problem. On the spot.

You can change things like store hours or store location or phone numbers right on the duplicate mechanical <u>before</u> you release it to those papers.

If your ad is going to run in a second paper and that paper does not have your type style, a duplicate of the mechanical sent to them will keep the same look going in all the papers you use.

The mechanical: who makes it?

In the near future, every newspaper may very well require complete mechanicals from retail stores. It's a question of time and economics. Theirs.

At present, mechanicals are prepared in three ways:

1. Many newspapers are now preparing mechanicals, especially papers printed by offset. You provide the layout, art, and copy. They set the type, make velox prints of the artwork and

combine all the graphic elements in a complete mechanical. They do this so they can send you a complete ad proof for your final approval.

Corrections are incorporated into the final mechanical, and then the ad is ready for the camera. This method has two weaknesses. First, the copy of the mechanical that you get may show all the elements in position, but it gives you no feeling of the tonal values of the ad. Secondly, when you make corrections, the newspaper may or may not make them on the mechanical. The next time you see the ad is in the paper. Too late to catch any errors of judgment or interpretation.

2. Other newspapers are now setting type, making velox prints from the artwork, then sending these back to the store. There the store's artists prepare the complete mechanical. This method takes staff time, but it's well worth it. Your management can see the complete ad, make adjustments, and approve details in the final stage before you release the ad to the paper.

3. Quite a number of stores . . . and this number is growing . . . are now doing it all themselves.

Setting their own phototypography or buying it outside.

Making their own velox prints or buying them outside.

Then preparing complete mechanicals, ready for camera.

This is the ideal. You get the type you want. You see your final corrections. You can examine your velox prints for interpretation of the art and for the way it will print. You can see your ad exactly as you want it. And you can expect to see it that way when you open your newspaper.

Working with the newspapers

We have always found newspapers cooperative. The ad representatives and the mechanical superintendents are all interested in having your ads look good . . . and sell more. It's their business, because the better your ads sell, the more space you'll buy.

They'll usually do everything they can (and their management lets them) to help solve your newspaper ad problems.

Except maybe a change of policy. Even then, if it's a matter of the paper's policy, discuss it with your ad representative, or the representative and the publisher together. They have been known to bend or change such policy. If it seriously affects their retail advertisers.

Most problems are not that serious. Your ad rep can answer questions like printing clarity, position in the paper, late proofs, typographic errors, and release dates. If he can't answer them himself, you'll get a specialist from the paper who can.

The advertising department's guardian angel at the newspaper is the mechanical superintendent. A very knowledgeable and very busy man.

He can tell you how to improve your art so that it will reproduce better.

He will help you get better veloxes.

He'll tell you what your layouts must have so the paper can do a better type job for you.

He'll watch out for . . . and watch over . . . a special ad and see that it gets special treatment.

He'll work with you when you have an ad emergency.

He will, naturally, be more interested in your ads if you show more interest. So get to know him. And use his expertise.

CHAPTER 12.

SALE ADS

Most sale advertising is dull and unconvincing. It usually sells numbers instead of benefits. It's often filled with unjustified and unsupportable superlatives.

Strong words? Take a look at your own newspaper.

Why is sale advertising so poor? Because most advertising people do not consider sale advertising creative.

They couldn't be more incorrect. It takes as much creativity to do a really good sale ad as any sprightly Merry Christmas institutional. Maybe more. We know. We've done both.

Next time you do a sale ad, don't just use a big word SALE and a big price . . . and let it go at that. Instead, tackle it as a special problem, a special kind of ad.

First, consider what a sale is. From the customer's point of view. A sale is getting more than you bargained for. Getting more than your money's worth. Paying less for something that would usually cost more.

It follows, then, that to do a convincing sale ad you must prove that what you're selling is worth more than your sale price. A comparative alone may not do it. If you say "reg. $20, now 14.99" . . . maybe it was over-priced at $20 to start off with. Maybe it's not even worth the 14.99. Our customers are getting to be very suspicious . . . and sophisticated . . . these days.

A good sale ad is convincing, urgent, and simple

The best way to convince readers is to give a reason for your sale. They know you're not in business to give things away. Provide a reason for your low price and you'll bridge the credibility gap.

And there often is a reason, if you dig hard enough. The merchant has made a special purchase, or you're overstocked, or you're taking inventory soon, or you're making way for new goods or a manufacturer has stopped cutting a line and is clearing his stock. Or you have a special sale event... with the reason built in. (We'll discuss that in a few paragraphs.)

Unfortunately... and with equal frequency... there is no solid reason. Except to beat last year's day.

In that case, latch on to the reason in the customer's mind... usually a seasonal need. "Swimsuit sale with lots of swimming weather ahead". "Sheet sale just when the family's coming for the holidays". "Raincoat sale in April? What better time!". You'll notice that these are specific. They avoid the generality trap of "most-wanted styles of raincoats". Which says nothing.

The other trap to avoid is the label headline. "Shirt Sale" is strictly a yawn. Either get a price story into the heading: "Save $2 on shirts now". Or an idea: "Every pair of polyester pants sale-priced". Or ask a question (it always gets the reader into the ad): "Why buy your winter coat in our August Coat Sale?". Or a fashion story: "The news in leisure jackets... sale-priced".

Urgency is obvious. Good ads have it. Good sale ads have lots of it. "Starting tomorrow". "3 days only". "Limited quantity". "Only 80 dresses at this price". "Last day".

You know these approaches. But don't stop there. Carry the urgency through the copy. "Be here when we open for the biggest buys". "Come early, come late, but don't miss this sale". "Why not buy your leather coat when our prices are so low?" "Come shop our sale of diamonds. A gem!" Think urgent, and urgency will appear in copy.

Believability, urgency, simplicity. A sale ad should be as simple and direct as you can make it. Gimmicks like explosions and flags and serried exclamation points actually distract from your message. Putting your sale heading in tricky type does not make it stronger. Let the facts tell your story. And keep those facts simple. The reason for the sale, the value story, the fashion story, and the urgency. In the most persuasive convincing language you can muster. Save your whimsey and your flights of fancy for other ads. Where there's not much to say.

With this in mind, let's examine the 2 basic sale ads.

The item sale and the sale event

In an item sale, you must sell the merchandise and the savings with equal emphasis.

If you had bread at a nickel a loaf, you wouldn't have to sell the advantages of bread at that price. The value is instantly communicable. But how often do you have an item like that? (Even then, you'd have a better ad if you explained that the bread was made from unbleached flour, with no additives, and shaped by loving hands.)

You must subtly explain why the item is worth more than your sale price. The turtle neck has a back zipper. The coat is made of fabric you'd expect only in expensive coats. The pants are super-fit. Designer sheets you've never seen for so little. The newest sweaters at a remarkable price.

In other words: give the customer benefits, the fashion story, then add the price story. To make the value convincing.

Never forget that, in a sale, the savings itself, is a major benefit. Don't just say "sale" and drop it. Keep reminding the reader that this is, indeed, an opportunity not to be missed.

The item sale is relatively simple. Compared to the sale event. When you can have a miscellany of everything from berets to bras under a single heading. The single umbrella heading, of course, is what makes the sale a sale event. Contrasted to a page of individual items at sale prices.

This umbrella has one great advantage. In itself, it gives a reason for the sale. January Coat Sale, After-Christmas Clearance, August White Sale, Anniversary Sale . . . even Founder's Day and Assistant Buyer's Day.

The communication is instant. They know that coats cost less during January Coat Sales. Nevertheless, a little explaining can

99

sometimes add a lot of pow. Was your founder a skinflint? A sharp trader? Dig into store history. Maybe you can justify your Founder's Day heading! An anniversary or birthday sale comes only once a year. Make hay of that.

If you're the biggest specialty shop or men's store or whatever in town, don't just have an After-Christmas Clearance. Have the biggest After-Christmas Fashion Clearance in town. Or before-the-4th-of-July sale. Not the biggest, but the best? Then how about the most fashionable After-Christmas Clearance in town? Again, a way of thinking, of getting away from labels.

If your sale event goes on for more than a week and slowly dies from lack of excitement, build mini-events into it. Have a special one-day sale in the middle. End with a grand finale.

The all-type sale ad

We believe in it. Firmly. Especially when you have an assortment of merchandise. The atmosphere sketch in a sale ad does nothing... except cost you money.

Type, properly used, can be just as dramatic... when the words are dramatic... as any piece of art. Actually it is the art.

If your sale is not limited to a specific item or items, and the art does nothing to enhance, to explain, or to sell... skip it. Don't waste your dollars.

We ought to warn you: every merchant wants art, even in the bloodiest sale, even if it's literally a thumb-nail spot. "How will they know it's a fashion sale if you don't show fashion", he'll wail. Well, if the words are right, they'll know. We've been through this, from liquor sales (nobody buys liquor because of the bottle... so why show it?) to shoe clearances (a little of this and a little of that). The atmosphere sketch does nothing except take valuable space. And all too often it weakens the ad.

The listing ad

Do people read listings? Yes. But more people will read more listings if you break up that solid gray mass of type.

100

You can break it up with headings. Sportswear. Coats. Lingerie.

You can break it up by boxing off some of your items.

You can break it up by going through your listings and pulling out a few that have a common denominator, then dramatizing them. For example, in an ad with 30 listings, there are 4 at 1/3 off. Lump them together with a "Save 1/3" heading. It will jump right out of the page.

If you have depth of stock, feature an item or items . . . with art.

You can even try running your headline across the middle or down the middle of your listings. Anything that makes the listing easier to read.

A few pointers:

The more is not the merrier, if more listings mean minuscule type. Use your normal size body type.

If you have a long gap between description and price, by all means use leaders. Better yet, shorten the gap.

Always end with your sale price. Opaque pantyhose, reg. 1.59, sale 89¢.

People have grown so accustomed to this that if you reverse it .... opaque pantyhose, sale 89¢, reg. 1.59 .... they'll think the sale price is 1.59.

Don't ask them to do arithmetic. Don't say . . . "Scarves, save 50%, reg. $2". They'll think . . . at least some of them . . . that the scarves are two bucks. Spell it out. "Save 50% on scarves. Reg. $2, now $1." This is particularly important when you have price ranges or odd numbers. Who's going to drag out the calculator to figure 1/3 off, reg. 22.98 to 31.69?

Comparatives and such

Let's start with the "and such". Should you say "50% off" or "half price"? "$2 off" or "10% off"? Psychologically, half price is always stronger than 50%. (Incidentally this is the exception to the "you" rule. "Half price" is stronger than "You save half".)

101

Some stores use both numerical and percentage savings. Add the regular and sale price and you've got a lot of numbers.

It's legitimate and honest to use whichever sounds like more. $2 off on a $20 item sounds like a good savings. 10% off $20 sounds picayune. So take the stronger way, and strengthen it further by translating "$2 off" to "Save $2".

What YOU do, instead of what WE are doing.

Comparative quotes, if used, must be honest and believable.

The honesty we leave to you and your store policy.

What's a believable quote? If your item is 63% less than last year's price, you might actually be better off dropping it a little. If the number is too big, it sounds as though you got stuck or the item's a dog. 50% seems to be the dividing line between believability and suspicion.

Should you use "regularly", "originally", "formerly" interchangeably? These words are self-explanatory. Regularly means that the merchandise will again be sold at the regular price after the sale. Follow FTC and Better Business Bureau guides.

There's a comparative expression not used often enough. Yet it's the most convincing way to phrase a comparative. Yesterday's price. Or last week's price. Use it if you can. It says quickly: this is regular stock. I would have paid more for it yesterday. I'm getting a bargain.

Some stores use no comparatives. How, then, do you get across the comparative value? By implication. Shop and compare. Why pay more? Look how much you get for so little. Imagine paying just $20 for this hand-made necklace. You've seen it advertised for lots more.

Note: If your store seems to have more and more sale events . . . question them. You may find that fewer and stronger events will add up to bigger dollar volume in the long run.

CHAPTER 13.

THE VENDOR-PAID AD

On September 12, 1975, one of our clients ran an ad for a special Hanes sale. In the same issue of the newspaper, a department store and another specialty shop had the same sale. All three used identical art, manufacture-supplied. Two of the three (not our client, we're glad to report), used tricky headline type and word-for-word copy. Again from Hanes.

Is this the way to make customers come running to <u>your</u> store? The answer is obvious.

This doesn't mean that you can't use vendor ads, or should turn down vendor money. But you must use them in your own way. As part of your advertising plan. In a style that's your style.

There are many forms in which co-op money, as it's often called, trickles into the advertising budget. The most common ones are:

a. The vendor or distributor provides mats (complete ads, ready to release to the paper). You may pay for part of the newspaper space or not, depending on what arrangements your merchants have made.

b. The vendor gives you an advertising allowance, a percentage against sales. The more of his goods you sell, the more money you get. You use this money to advertise his products.

c. The manufacturer pays for an ad, or pays part, when you send him a tear sheet of the ad as proof of performance.

These arrangements are made by merchants when they're out buying. How you get the money is not as important as how well you use it.

Merchants love vendor money. As they should. It lets them expose more merchandise in the papers. In their enthusiasm, however, they often promise the moon .. and a couple of other

103

satellites ... in exchange. Things like the vendor's name at the top of the page, or the largest type on the page. Or using his logo. Or getting 92 items into an ad. Or language that doesn't belong in a retail ad ... or is contrary to your store policy.

This can become such a problem that many stores now require merchants to submit contracts to the ad department for approval before they sign them.

Note: These contracts are usually standard forms. The vendor wants to get as much as he can. You can't blame him. But you'd be surprised how often a requirement will be changed. If you say you can't meet it.

What's the best way to use vendor money?

By creating an ad so characteristic of your store that only you and the vendor know that it's vendor-paid. This is better for both of you ... because you'll both do more business on it. An ad that talks to your customer in her language, to her interests. And in your ad style, in your type face. Your ad.

If the art in a mat or a glossy is better than you can afford, by all means use it. Just make sure that, if you're using it in an ad with other art work, they work together.

But change the language. Start from scratch, and write your own ad and design it as though you were paying for it. Noting, and honoring, your committments to the vendor.

Why is this important?

First of all, any ad a manufacturer produces must, of necessity, be general. Not only doesn't he know your customer, but his prose must appeal to millions of women. With widely varying life styles. Sure, your audience may run from militant young executive persons to homebodies, but the manufacturer probably sends the same stuff to a store whose customers are retired sheep ranchers and a store in a college town.

There is also a vital difference between the function of a national ad and a retail ad. A manufacturer is, basically, selling his name.

He wants you to remember it ... and when you're in the market for his product, you'll ask for it by name. At some time. At any store.

A retail ad, on the other hand, wants you to come in tomorrow ... and buy this item at this store.

That's why, if you pick up the vendor copy, you'll have a weak ad. It will talk about him. Not about you and your customer.

Fortunately, some vendors are enlightened. All they ask is that you do a good ad. They'll send you loads of literature, of course, to prime you. Beware. This gun is loaded. With superlatives that need examining. With trade talk that needs cleaning up.

Let's take the superlatives first. The manufacturer has only one product or a limited group of products to sell. When he says: the best-fitting pantyhose or suit, he's merely boasting. When you make that kind of statement, consider what you are actually saying about the 8 other brands of pantyhose you sell, the scores of other suits on your rack. That they don't fit well?

Superlatives are never good copy. They can also be dangerous.

As for trade lingo. If you don't understand it, your customer surely won't. Don't just pick it up literally. Translate it into plain English or explain it.

Do you know what a "rope shoulder" is on a man's suit? Neither do we, but we saw it in an ad recently. Along with "1/3 lined". Which third?

Watch out, too, for trade talk. Like "from our line of". Customers don't think "line". Manufacturers and their salesmen do. Customers think "collection of", "assortment of", "array of", even "dazzle of". But not "line".

How much VP advertising should you run?

As we said, co-op money sweetens the pot and stretches your own advertising dollars. So far so good. But, like all freebies, there are pitfalls.

105

Are you running ads on merchandise that is not up to your standards, or not typical of your store ... merely because there's money to pay for this advertising? What kind of impression does this make on the reader?

Are you often in the paper only with vendor-paid ads? Without, at the same time, exposing the merchandise you'd run if you had the money? This can give the reader a very cockeyed view of what your store stands for.

Shortly after World War II, when we were both at Bamberger's, housewares were pretty scarce, and so was vendor money. But Sherwin Williams paint, Renuzit, and some silver polish whose name we forget, had plenty of goods ... and money to match. So every Sunday, the Bam's housewares ad .. the only housewares ad .. was some combo of the 3. A whole page. Sunday after Sunday. We sure looked like a cleaning store instead of New Jersey's greatest housewares department.

There was nothing wrong with the merchandise. It was fine merchandise. But too narrow a category to represent a whole department, week after week.

So before you spend all those vendor dollars, take a look how they affect the merchandise mix you're presenting to the reader.

It's a good idea to check results, too. You may find that you're getting a very poor response to vendor-paid ads. It may be that your ads are not effective. That you can fix. But if the merchandise is not what your customers want or the prices are wrong, you'd be better off without those ads.

See pages 169 and 170 for suggested cooperative advertising agreements for use by store executives.

CHAPTER 14.

THE MAIL AND PHONE AD

Traditionally, the specialty shop has not solicited mail and phone business. For many reasons. Limited depth of stock, for one. The feeling that, in a fashion store, customers want to come in and see and try on. The fear of returns. The desire to build traffic for unadvertised items and trade up when the customer does come in. Plus inexperience and lack of systems for handling mail and phone orders.

These <u>were</u> all sound reasons. Then why are more and more specialty stores actively looking for mail and phone business these days?

Because now even the most elegant shops carry certain items that can be classed as staples. After all, you don't have to see the merchandise to order a favorite style of pantyhose. Or Bali bra. Or white Van Heusen shirt. Or Fieldcrest towel. Even classic pull-on slacks and turtlenecks. Even some jewelry. And so forth.

With the right kind of ad, you can sell almost anything by mail and phone. Take shoes. Some shoe stores do a huge mail order business. Since, in our observation, most copywriters have funny feet, this may come as a surprise to you. Apparently there are enough people who know that if they order the size they wear, the shoe will fit. Without trying on 20 different pairs to find one that's comfortable.

Mail and phone business is on the increase. Why? The soaring price of gas and public transit has made shopping at home thriftier. Larger and larger numbers of women are working; they don't have time to shop. Moreover, today's customer is sophisticated and knowledgeable. She pretty well knows what she wants when she sees it in the newspapers.

No wonder there are stores (mainly department stores) that keep their switchboards open 24 hours a day, 7 days a week.

Much of this business is plus business; sales the store would not make if customers had to come in. And who doesn't like plus business?

How do you get your share? By tacking a "mail and phone orders accepted" to the end of an ad? Well, that may stir a few people to action. You'd do far better if you decided in advance that this is a mail and phone item and write your ad with that in mind. Especially if it's mail order. Which we'll explain in a moment.

If you want people to buy sight unseen, you must make sure your ad includes all the facts necessary to make a buying decision. Generalities are bad copy in any ad. They're a disaster in mail and phone ads. Nobody can order "summer fashion colors". Or even "misses sizes".

You must provide all the facts that do not show in the picture. Colors, sizes, fabric, fibre content. Naturally. But how about the shirred back yoke that doesn't show? The convertible cuff? The tapered fit? The square cut bottom tucked into a skirt? The size of a handbag? Small and big are non-descriptive when you don't have them in hand.

Spell all this out. Then make it easy for the customer to order. If you're not set up to handle COD's, say "Sorry, no COD's". If she must add sales tax, tell her so. If there's a delivery charge, don't bury it. (In some states delivery charges must be displayed next to the price.)

If you don't, you may spend a lot of money on postage, returning those nice orders and checks.

Phone orders

Since a customer can talk to someone, presumably her questions can be answered. If all you want are phone orders, you _can_ skip little clutter-bugs like "matching buttons". You don't have to ask for 2nd color choice. Your order taker will know when mauve's

108

gone. She can also tell her about another smashing sweater if you run out of the advertised one. And figure the sales tax for her.

The basic requirement for a phone ad is elementary: your phone number. In good size type, where the customer can find it. Including your area code if your newspaper reaches outside your area.

Who takes the phone order? In some stores, the switchboard operator is also the order taker. She has current ads in front of her, plus any supplementary material the buyer feels the customer might want.

In other stores, order calls are switched to the floor, to sales people. This has the advantage of bringing calls to those who know the merchandise. It also gums up service when the floor is busy. A happy compromise is to suggest that the customer call when you're not so busy. "Phone orders, of course. But not between noon and 2". Or "afternoons only".

No store worthy of its shingle has to be told about the beauty of what a man we worked for used to call "suggestive selling". Once you have a live customer at the other end of the wire. However, your suggestions will work better if your advertising department writes some suggested copy . . . with sell . . . to be used by those who take orders. Especially if your switchboard operator is doubling as the phone order board. Most sales people can wing it. After all, selling is their job. Not the switchboard operator's.

The exception is account solicitation. Anyone who takes phone orders . . . and this includes the boss . . . must be reminded, entreated, exhorted to try to open a charge account for every customer who does not have one. The advertising department should prepare a list of the advantages of an account in clear, simple, good English. Otherwise you may get a lot of hemming and hawing and involved, clumsy language that will lose the customer in mid-stream.

From time to time, your store may decide to include a message with the answering "hello". Blah & Blah, your merry Christmas store. Blah & Blah, your fashion store. Blah & Blah, where it's

Spring Sale time. This language, too, should originate in the advertising department.

Mail orders

Here copy and illustration must, between them, answer every question a customer might ask. You must also keep poetic license to an absolute minimum. This is no place for exaggeration. Not even the slightest.

If, for example, you let your prose run away with you, and call a quilted jacket thick and puffy . . . and it turns out to be skinny and droopy . . . all you'll get are returns. Expensive returns. Ditto if you call a fabric shiny which only has a nice dull sheen. So temper your adjectives. You can write good exciting selling copy and stick to the literal facts. It just takes more thought.

Again, like phone order copy, the basic requirement is to make it easy for the customer to order. That means your address, complete with zip code. So they can read it and find it. You'd be startled at how many stores assume customers know where they are. They forget that many loyal intelligent customers know exactly how to get to a store . . . without knowing its street address.

Should you use coupons? That depends. If the item is simple, communicable, you have lots of it, and can afford the space, you'll probably get more business from a coupon than from asking for mail orders. A coupon makes it simpler to order . . . and most people are lazy. Also a coupon in an ad says very quickly "Order me by mail".

But beware of several things.

1. We have rarely seen coupons that are big enough to use comfortably. Not everybody can write on the head of a pin or is named Smith. If you're going to spend the space for a coupon, what's the point of making it so small it can't be used? Try filling it out yourself, if you have any doubts.

2. If you have more than one item in an ad, make sure copy and art are so explicitly keyed that there is no possible confusion.

3. Watch out for the second color choice bit. Buyers love it. It protects them from deciding which color will move best. They'll put it in even when they have a million in each color. Your customer may not care whether her sale-priced cotton panties are pink or white. But if she wants a blue shirt, she wants a blue shirt, not a yellow one. If you ask for second color choice, she may decide not to order at all. So question second color choice in a coupon. And first, second, and third choice when there are only three colors. You'll discourage orders.

4. Make sure your coupon includes all the information your store needs to fill an order. Quantity, size, item, color, price, tax, charge account number. Plus things like length if you have proportioned pants. Patterns if you have plaids and stripes. Look at the merchandise to anticipate customer questions.

Postscript

Don't be satisfied with always saying "write or phone" or "mail and phone orders accepted". If you have space, go creative. Incidentally, this may be the easiest way to even out a copy block.

Phone orders? We love them.

Write for your new sweater today.

Mail and phone, of course.

We're waiting to hear from you by mail or phone. Or come see us.

To make it easy, we've included a coupon. Why not use it now?

This will make your ad a lot livelier. And, we think, get you extra business.

CHAPTER 15.

SPECIAL EVENTS
AND HOW TO PROMOTE THEM

The purpose of an event is to build traffic. If it doesn't do this, markedly, who needs the trouble?

In order to build traffic, of course, you have to tell the public what's happening. A little line buried in an ad won't do it. You must dramatize the event in order to get attention. You can actually make an event seem far bigger and more exciting than it is. And convince people.

For a major event, use every sales promotion property at your disposal.

Advertising: buy the necessary extra space and time to get your story across. Then steal space from ads for an editorial. Use baselines. Use headlines. Anything and everything to reinforce the impression.

Then add window signs and posters, before the event as well as during it. Bill enclosures (if the event is for a limited time, watch that cycle billing). Press releases, with pictures. Even the indicia on your postage meter!

Your anniversary

It happens every year. Like Christmas, Mother's Day, and annual clearances, it's something you can start planning the minute this year's event is over. And should.

Most stores have a birthday sale. Which is not a bad way to celebrate. It's a fine umbrella. People expect extraordinary bargains when they see the anniversary or birthday sale heading. Just don't drag it out too long. It's better to have a sizzler going for one week than a tepid sale for three. Concentrate your advertising.

That way everybody and her sister will know you've a sale.

This is the time to buy 10 second spots (ID's .... see chapter 18). Lots of them. To spread the news. And even if you don't usually use TV, it's a good investment to have a timeless TV spot developed for the sale. You can use it for years, amortizing its cost.

Do you need an institutional, talking about your anniversary, your history, your sale? Only if it's _very_ very good and clever. There's no bigger bore than a picture of Our Founder and Our Original Store. You're better off putting the money in merchandise advertising.

But what if you decide you don't want an anniversary sale?

Create your own event, your own excitment.

One fascinating route is via nostalgia.

Let's say it's your 34th anniversary. Go to your newspapers and have stats made of front pages 34 years ago. Go through your files. You may find your opening ad! Get your local historical society into the act. Write to Women's Wear Daily and ask for fashion material. See if your radio station has old tapes. Old songs, old movies, old records .... the list is limited only by your imagination. Let it soar.

What if you're only 11 or 12, with no nostalgia value? Have a week of little "give-aways". A dozen bats to the Little League. A dozen seedling trees to the local park. A dozen books to the library. Etc. There's publicity mileage in all this.

Incidentally, the round numbers are the time for the biggest noise about an anniversary .... 5, 10, 25, 50, 100.

The fashion show

If you're going to the expense of mounting a fashion show, promote it for all it's worth.

Informal modeling. Doing it? Then flaunt it. Take a big headline. At the top, middle, or bottom of your ad. Or even all three.

"INFORMAL FASHION SHOW ALL DAY TOMORROW".
Or build the story into a merchandise headline "See these jump-suits informally modeled tomorrow afternoon".

The fashion show you're invited to give. The group that invites you is responsible for getting the bodies into the little gold chairs. But it's a nice gesture to add a reminder in your advertising.

Your own fashion show. Here it's up to you to build audience. Via newspaper, radio, store signs, calls or notes to customers. Don't start too far in advance, or they'll forget the date (exception: ticketed shows, then 2 weeks is none too soon). On the other hand, give them a little time to plan. Like 3 days.

One of our clients, a specialty shop in a college town, in coopera-tion with a men's store, pulled an audience of 3000 for a fashion show in the park. You read that right. 3000. How did they do it? By taking the first real center spread the local newspaper had ever done, including the "gutter", the center column. (All vendor-paid!) By saturating radio. By taking ads in the college news-paper. By publicity. Phone calls. Ballyhoo and all that stuff.

Does it pay to advertise? It certainly does!

Opening a new department or new store

This is one time you don't have to create news. It's there. When you say "Opening tomorrow". So think big, and act big.

A new department or a remodeled one may require only an ad or series of ads. Plus a press release. But a new store, or an addition to your store, is a once-in-a-while chance to make an impression bigger than the event itself. If you do it with drama.

Here are sone of the things you can do.... just to start you thinking.

Press party and private preview for account customers or any other group you want to favor. You can combine these effec-tively. It's better for the press to see a "working" store than an empty one. Naturally, you'll have a press kit ready.

Breakfast for staff: the inspirational message.

Ribbon cutting by your mayor or other celebrity. Only don't make it a ribbon.

A teaser ad and radio spots every day the week before opening. Hinting at what's coming.

Opening ad and follow-up ads. With merchandise. And all the excitement of a new place for people to explore and enjoy and admire and shop.

Live coverage by your local radio station on opening day. Then radio spots to follow up the opening.

A "success story" ad the day after opening (prepared, of course, way in advance), thanking everybody. You'll never have another chance to do this!

Account solicitation. Before you open, if you can afford it. Certainly a special desk to open accounts on the spot opening day.

Bill enclosure. Tell your customers what's happening. Even if it's a new store and they don't live in the area. It proves that you're going places.

Gifts for opening day or week. Limited only by your funds and your influence on vendors. One of the nicest gifts is a special shopping bag. It will be carried around and keep working for you!

Fashion shows: big, little, or in-between. You'll draw maximum crowds to your opening, so expose as much merchandise at that time as you can.

Drawing for prizes. Because it gets more people into the act, it's better to have a lot of little prizes rather than one big one. Try not to give away goods you sell. It deters buying. They wait to see who won. Hold the drawing after peak traffic days and hours.

Demonstrations. Cosmetics, wigs, scarf-tying, even yoga exercises. Anything to make the store live and lively.

You take it from here. Always planning well in advance. Shopping bags, for example, can take months to print.

Contests, giveaways, demonstrations, tie-ins, etc.

Once again, they're worth the effort only if they result in extra traffic. Don't flatter yourself that a line at the end of a copy block in a single ad will do it. Either buy space or steal space for a box. If what you're promoting is related to the merchandise in the ad, make it part of your headline. That's the news, isn't it?

Planning events

Since an event is not usually dreamed up overnight, don't wait till it appears on the schedule. Pre-plan. There are few satisfactions that can match having an event on proof weeks before it has to run. If, for some reason, you can't prepare the actual properties, you can certainly have your thinking done in advance.

With the exception of events so small they require no props and a single ad, each event needs a "responsiblity" sheet. Who's going to do what to whom, when and where. This eliminates buck-passing, alibis, and a lot of last minute scurrying.

You make a list of everything that must be done and when it should be ready on one side, then fill in the name of the person who's supposed to get it done on the other side.

You will find a simple form in the Appendix that you can use for this purpose. To be elaborated on, if you wish. For you can spell out just the basic facts or go into great detail.

Who should issue such an information sheet? And control it? The person running the event. Publicity, if you have such a department. The advertising director. Or even the store president. If this kind of thing is his bag. As long as you have the responsibilities for each and every detail in writing. With someone to mother-hen it and make sure what's required is ready when it's required.

CHAPTER 16.

DIRECT MAIL

Direct mail is a big subject. It covers everything from a postcard to a giant catalogue in full color. But certain truths hold for each and every one of them.

A customer does not buy from a mailing piece. She buys from a store. You must project your store's personality, talk to your customer. She must know that it comes from you. Not just because your name is on it, but because it looks and sounds like you.

Direct mail is expensive. To produce. To print. To mail. It must pay its way by bringing a maximum return for every item.

All the principles of good copy and good graphics apply. That means your direct mail must be dramatic, readable, easy to shop from. It should give the customer benefits, the news, the reasons for shopping your store, be topical, timely, and always always talk "you".

Direct mail frees you from the clutter of competition you find in the newspaper, as we said when we discussed media. But there are other clutters to consider. These days we all get advertising mail by the pound. That's why it's a bright idea to mail first class whenever you can. Obviously it's not good economics to send a 120-page catalogue first class. But a small folder and every letter ... anything under an ounce, should travel in style.

And don't clutter your customers with your own mailings. If you go to the same well too often, you know what happens. An endless stream of mailings? Reconsider them. Can some be eliminated? The vendor sale that doesn't pull its weight? The traditional event that might be better in the newspapers? Or can you consolidate some? This may mean changing your time table. Which is often good for the soul .. and the store as well.

Lists

Fundamentally, a mailing is only as good as your list. Maybe you can sell ice cubes to Eskimos, but even the most superb mailing will sell very few coats to those women who bought their coats last month.

Lists start with your charge account customers. They're your steadies. Loyal, constant, and also tied to you by the convenience of being able to charge what they buy. If you want to expand your list, where do you go?

You can buy lists, but buying a list should be a last resort. You usually get too much dead wood on such a list to justify an expensive mailing.

Start with your list of customers. We assume you keep one. Every time you have a contest or a free gift offer, take names off the entry blanks. Check on your computer. Not on your list? Then add them.

You can get lists of brides and new residents from your newspapers (the former) and your bank (the latter).

If you give a fashion show to a charity group, make one of your conditions for giving the show the names and addresses of all members.

A college nearby? There are student lists, usually for the asking. If not, try taking an ad in the college paper, and get the list in return. You might even do business on the ad!

If there are women's clubs and professional groups in the area, call the secretary. Tell her you have a special offer for her members you'd like to mail out. This should earn you the list.

Then re-examine your own lists and use them intelligently. We've discovered that even small computers can do wonders. Provided you can persuade those who run the computer to bother. The computer can "burst" any kind of list, with the proper programming. Customers who shop only the junior department, so you won't send them notices of half-size sales. And vice-versa.

118

A classic example of pin-pointing an audience is an ad for hearing aids that's run for generations. The headline asks "Are you deaf?" Take a cue from that.

In these days of expensive mailings, you may want to do small pin-pointed pieces, rather than try to hit everyone. With the help of your computer. Customers who buy bras, girdles, or anything else where fit is a problem ... from pantyhose to proportioned sizes ... are natural repeats. And candidates for small mailings. Or those who bought your ski clothes or tennis clothes last year. Use your imagination. And your lists. You won't make new customers this way, but chances are you'll get a fantastic return for your direct mail dollars.

Postcards, letters, and such

Have you ever read a card or letter actually written by a buyer or salesperson? Or even the boss? It's for real, all right, because it's almost invariably clumsy, wordy, and trite. That kind of reality you don't need.

Everything that goes out in the mail should come out of the advertising department. Even the little note your star saleswoman sends to her customers when a new shipment of goodies arrives. We are the professionals. We know how to sell in words.

Postcards are no problem. Space limits what you can say, so just give the facts as briefly and pleasantly as you can. A signature is a nice personal touch. The kind that brings in business.

Note: Buying offices often prepare out-size cards for their clients. The annual after-Easter clearance, the store-wide sale, and events they dream up. These cards are relatively cheap. But cheap is expensive when they don't do the job well. Like all general messages, these cards are too general to work effectively for any individual store. Pay the extra few bucks to have the type re-set, and write your own story. If you can then have it set in your own type face, so much the better. (This may be difficult; the buying office gets a bulk rate from a printer. He may not have your type face.) You'll find this pays off. In sales. In reinforcing the total impression you make.

119

Letters can be a beautiful vehicle for selling. If you write the right kind of letter. What's that? A me-to-you letter, because the letter, of all mailings, is the most personal.

Be friendly, be chatty, be informal. Use postscripts for emphasis, use underlining (in another color if you can afford it), use caps ... but always be natural. Every letter should be signed. By a person. Not "Store XX". Not "Dress Department". But X.X. Xavier, President. J.J. Jones, Dress Buyer.

If it goes out under the boss's signature, be particularly careful with your approach and your language. The boss doesn't talk about petty little details. He's supposed to think big. (Whether he does or not.) He might prattle on about the size and scope of your umbrella sale, but he wouldn't spell out the four different kinds of fabric combinations.

Long lists within a letter are fatal. Guaranteed to stop the reader from reading on. Even when you think you're being very clever and paragraph them. If you must have a list, it belongs on another sheet of paper, or even the back of your letter.

Try to avoid the tired old cliches in the opening sentence. "It is our pleasure", "We invite you", "We thought you'd like to know".

Instead, be interesting, be provocative, be warm. "As you know, we've had some remarkable sales in the past, but". "If you think it's a long time until you'll get into a bathing suit". "Here's some happy news".

How long should a letter be? As long as necessary to tell the story and convince the reader. Like any other piece of copy. You're probably familiar with what's become known as the "Book Of The Month Club" style letter. It runs on for four pages, with lots of short paragraphs and underlined phrases. This type of letter has been intensively tested. It works. It works because it's written like a cliff-hanger. Each paragraph leads you inevitably to the next. The reader can't stop reading.

This doesn't mean you should indulge in a lot of unnecessary prose. (Our own Parkinson's law is that words fill the space vacant for them.) But when you do have a real story to tell, insist on enough space to tell it in. Then tell it well and interestingly.

Does a letter need a gimmick to generate response? If you have a good gimmick, you'll find it works particularly well in a letter. A private preview. A postscripted sale item just for them. A pair of tickets to a private sale or a special discount. That kind of thing. Only don't give the store away. We think it's most unfortunate that some specialty stores invite their best customers... their charge accounts ... to a private event, then proceed to give their own merchandise as door prizes. You don't need to. You deter sales. Even if you get the goods free from vendors, this is bad psychology.

Booklets, catalogues, and such

These are major efforts, major mailings. If you can swing them on your own, great. If you must rely heavily on vendor money, not so great. Why? Because there's no free lunch. Vendor paid merchandise is rarely the newsiest, the most exciting. Or the merchandise you'd put in a booklet if you didn't have to consider dollars. Look at Christmas booklets across the country, as we have. Year after year, you find nice solid undramatic merchandise, because most are vendor supported. On the other hand, no vendor money, no booklet.

There are two ways off the horns of this dilemma. One is to use all the dollars you can get, then spice your booklet with interesting unusual items and pay for these yourself. It could make the whole booklet come alive. The other is to work with ideas. Don't do a conventional booklet. Group merchandise by price (gifts under $10, under $20 ... that's the way people buy anyway) or by natural buying patterns (robes and slippers on the same page, long dresses and evening bags). These are simple devices. You can probably dream up a dozen as good or better. All you need is one to transform any booklet from strictly so-what to wow!

Your buying office may peddle booklets that they prepare. Nice booklets with your logo, your editorial, and small changes of prices and sizes to accomodate each store. Just be warned. If these booklets make you buy merchandise you wouldn't otherwise ... or find hard to sell ... or depth of stock in narrow categories that swallows up your open-to-buy for months ... forget it. It's bad news. You're better off with your not so glossy book. Or none.

What do you do when your competition is a giant store that rolls out a great big gorgeous Christmas catalogue in full color? Break the bank trying to match them? That's crazy. Go elegant and quiet instead. Buy a rich heavy paper folder that will fit into your standard envelope. Put your jolly message on the cover. Then fill the folder with single sheets. Each with a picture and heading on one side, copy and coupon on the other. Saks 5th Avenue has been doing this for years. They call it their Folio and it's an attractive, relatively inexpensive way to expose merchandise.

Special direct mail techniques

Because there are usually many items to a page and space is at a premium, most direct mail is designed first, then copy is written to the layout. What you ... designer, copywriter, or typographic expert ... must keep reminding yourself is this. In direct mail, you don't have to compete with other ads. You don't need huge art, screaming headlines, gigantic prices. Everything scales down.

Also ... a booklet is not a series of single ads. There must be a family relationship from page to page. In graphics. In ideas. Your booklet should be consistent, even in its variations. So it adds up to a single whole.

The cover. Unlike the contents of the booklet, this does compete. With other mail. It should be dramatic. It's your one chance to make the customer look inside. If you can't afford superb art or a magnificent photo, use beautiful type. Whichever you use, however, stay away from labels. "New Spring Fashions from Store XX" is about as newsy as last year's gossip. "Spring Sale at Store XX" names the event. Without any come-hither.

Let's take those two ideas and see what can be done to them.

122

Isn't it wonderful to shed your
winter coat and get into Spring?
Fashion News from Store XX

Spring goes on Sale April 3 at precisely 10 a.m.
Come gather bargains by the armful
at Store XX

Headings. Forget the 3 or 4 word page heading, and write what are really short editorials for some pages. Remember, you don't need big type. Editorials about fashion ideas, the store, your services. Do you need your name in every heading? No. Once in a while is enough.

For your traditional headings, avoid generalities. Like "Spring Dress-up Time" or "Smart Separates for Everyone". They merely eat up space and say nothing. Maybe you don't need a heading. When you have merchandise so wildly assorted that you really have to dig for a common denominator, skip it. Do a heading on a store superiority, store hours, charge accounts or other service.

Items. Write benefit headings for the individual items. Then keep your copy succinct, but do include all the facts the reader needs in order to buy. Not enough space? Then scream. Either the merchandise is wrong for the space (buyers should be taught that if they must have 6 items described and show a picture, this can't be done in 2 square inches; they should request larger space) or you need a revised layout.

This is not a license to let loose with adjectives and poetic imagery. If your customer benefit headline is a good strong one, all you need are facts. Spelled out. Not "Spring colors", but "Spring blue, pink, beige, white". Avoid strange abbreviations to save space. SML are OK. Customers have learned what they mean. But not bl/wh/pur/gr. Don't ask them to work. They won't.

Sale. If your direct mail is a sale booklet, keep the sale concept going. Keep reminding them that this is a rare chance to save money. You can't say it often enough. Then, as in any good piece

123

of sale copy, point out why the merchandise is worth more than your asking price.

Keying. Unless you have each block of copy under the art, both art and copy should be keyed. Simply. 1,2,3,4 or a,b,c,d are the clearest. If there's no possibility of confusion, left to right is equally clear. But don't go tricky. Clockwise and counterclockwise for example, raise the question ... where do you start?

Bill enclosures

Mostly these are supplied by vendors. With your name imprinted.

We believe that most specialty stores are not choosy enough.

Think about it for a moment. You are actually lending a vendor your best customer list ... and your best mailing (nobody ignores a charge account bill). Make sure you get something out of it.

Don't load up your bill envelope with merchandise that's marginal. In style. In workmanship. Or potential return. Remember, you'll have to stock the stuff.

Even if the enclosure passes the merchandise test, read it carefully. Is it right for you? Or does it make statements ... or promises ... you wouldn't make in your own ads? Unfortunately, you can't get most vendors to change their bill enclosures. But you can always say no. It's better to have your bill envelope travel light than load it up with the wrong things. Merely because you get the enclosures free.

CHAPTER 17.

SIGNS: INSIDE AND OUT

Should merchants write their own signs? The answer is one word: no. Ditto for the display department.

Like any other communication to the customer, signs should come out of the advertising department. Out of a copywriter's typewriter.

Why? Because it's the copywriter's job to translate information into customer language. And, at the same time, reflect the personality of your store.

Window signs

A window sign is unlike any other advertising property. It's not an ad. It is not a poster. Instead, it's a brief news story. An editorial comment on the contents of the window. Its sole function is to tell the passerby enough about the merchandise to make her come into the store. Since the customer can't buy from the window, you can skip a lot of the details. After all she can see the merchandise.

The window sign is one of the few exceptions to the rule about generalities. They work well in windows because they can be used to summarize and editorialize.

If you have good name brands, use them. If it's been shown in a magazine, boast a little. Third party endorsement is always good sales talk.

Make sure you give the essentials. Size category (juniors, young men, etc.). Where she can find it in the store. And prices. Customers want to know what things cost. Especially these days. Some people are timid. If it looks expensive .... and we assume your display department will make even a $5 sweater look expensive .... they may not even come in and ask how much.

Management or the display department may think prices clutter up the window and the sign. OK. Put prices on a small card. A window without prices is like an ad without prices. A dumb way to use space.

You'll be glad to know that if you have a penchant for puns, a window sign is probably the best place to use them. Because a sign gets a passing glance instead of an in-depth analysis.

And always, be as brief as you can.

Interior signs

Perhaps your store believes that signs on the counters or around the floor bug up the place. They're right. But there are times when signs are necessary. As guide-posts for the customer. To call attention to advertised goods or a special they mightn't otherwise be aware of.

Writing copy for interior signs is simple: just keep it direct, factual, informative. Skip anything that can be quickly seen: the merchandise will be right there. No adjectives, unless they're descriptive. No fine and fancy prose. No long explanations. If the merchandise needs a lot of explanation, let the sales clerks do it. That's what they're there for. A sign is no place to tell people how to use something. It's a selling vehicle, not a demonstration.

Most of all, be brief but informative. Don't write labels. Don't say "Handbags $10". Say something about the bags. "The new soft vinyls $10". "Leather-lined bags at a surprising $20".

What if you have a lot of facts? First, eliminate. Use only the most vital ones. Then bullet your facts. Complete sentences take too many words.

Suggestion: You can save yourself a lot of fussing, if you have special "As advertised" and "Sale" toppers designed to slip on top of your sign frame. These get attention, especially if you use color.

Posters

A poster is a graphic device to catch the customer.

It is, basically, a beautifully designed headline.... and should have no more words than you use in a heading. If you need more words, make sure that a few words can be dramatized. If you can use color, great.

Posters are for only the simplest of messages: "Storewide Spring Sale". "Open an account today". "Open late every night till Christmas". "Have you seen our new suit shop?".

What's the difference between a sign and a poster? A poster is bigger. It does not refer to merchandise right near it. It is "designed" or hand-lettered.It can contain graphics. And usually remains in place far longer than a sign. In fact, if it's a good one, you can use it year after year. Repainting when the ivy starts twining around it. Or it starts to look shabby.

Sign information

If you don't already have such a system, you should develop a "request for sign" information sheet. You will find a form for this kind of sheet in the Appendix. To embroider, depending on what the display department and the advertising department need.

When you have a form, it becomes routine for the merchant to fill it out when he has a window display or interior sign coming up. And routine for the writer to write it and send it on to the display department, instead of a last-minute crisis when the window is already dressed, or the advertised merchandise is on the floor.

CHAPTER 18.

RADIO

Most retailers have grown up in a world of print. They think print. But most of their customers have grown up tuned into radio.

It's only fairly recently that the gap has been bridged. That specialty stores have invaded the air waves to compete with used car dealers, airlines, and fast food outlets. Because they feel it's an unfamiliar medium, many of them have been letting their radio stations write commercials for them. Nonsense.

Anyone who can write a good print ad can write a good radio ad. The technique is different, that's all. Radio ads should be done by the regular advertising people. Who know the store. If you want to sound like yourself . . . rather than the local drive-in.

But they must be radio ads. You can't retype a newspaper ad verbatim on clean white paper . . . and expect it to be an effective radio commercial. You must rewrite it for the air, because it's a different medium with different requirements.

How does a radio ad differ from a newspaper ad?*

1. There is no stopper, no big headline or art. *You must get the listener's attention with words.*

2. The ear is less attentive than the eye. Reading takes full concentration, but you can listen with half an ear. That's why you must *repeat, repeat, repeat.*

3. Listeners can't go back to figure out what you mean. *So keep your sentences simple, brief,uncomplicated.*

4. There's no logotype to identify your store. Don't leave them wondering where they can get it. *Tell them again and again.*

---

*Adapted from "Retail Advertising Copy: the How, the What, the Why" by Judy Young Ocko, published by the NRMA.

5. You have no picture to support your prose. If there are important facts, *you must give word pictures.*

6. Words that look right don't always sound right and some combinations of words make for stumbling. *Read your commercials out loud.*

7. *Your audience can't absorb and remember a lot of numbers.* Don't try to give 3 prices, a phone number, and an extension in 30 seconds.

8. *The announcer is not a spokesman for the store,* but a third party. When he talks about your store, it's "they", not "we". If it's live. If <u>you</u> tape, you can talk "we" or even "I".

9. *You have only one chance to attract an audience ...* with your lead-in. If you don't catch them then, they'll turn off their ears.

Where do you start?

If you're turning an ad into a commercial, you start with the ad. Otherwise with a complete information sheet and the merchandise. The list of customer benefits, all the facts, any store superiorities. Then to the typewriter. To develop a lead-in.

On radio, an intriguing lead-in is crucial. Most people don't really start listening... until you stop them. Then they tune in and absorb the rest of your message.

Your lead-in can be news, or a benefit, or a question, or something topical or even whimsical. As long as it stops them. For example ... and we think you can identify the merchandise without being told even though the lead-ins are indirect. As they should be.

Do your shoes spend more time in the closet than on your feet?

The next 30 seconds could make you look good on the tennis court, so listen carefully.

If you're worried about the cost of living ... and aren't we all?

It's an unwritten law. When you want to wear your prettiest clothes, it rains.

129

There's a new fashion arithmetic you ought to learn. It's called separates.

When you've raced around all day in pants, you deserve something lovely to come home to.

Are you turning your thermostat down to 68°?

Once you have your lead-in... on with the copy. Repeating important facts. Customer benefits. Store name. Price. As often as you can.

How many words?

Radio time is usually bought as 10-second spots, also known as ID's (Identifications), 30 seconds, and one minute.

You can get 25 to 30 words in an ID, about 75 in 30 seconds, and 150 in a minute.That's wall-to-wall with words. Short words. If you have polysyllabics, (which you shouldn't) they take longer to say. If you have music, that eats up part of the time, too.

A stop watch makes timing accurate. And don't try to kid yourself by reading fast. In print, if you have too many words you can always reduce the type size. On the air, you end up with a breathless announcer racing to make it. Hardly a selling climate.

In an ID, your store name should be mentioned twice... in a 30-second spot, 3 times... in a minute 4 or more times. If you can get extra mentions in gracefully, good!

Some tips

Except possibly in the lead-in, there's no place in radio copy for generalities. You don't have the words to spare on them. You must be specific. Like the radio announcer. Who doesn't say "cold tomorrow" but "28° tomorrow". You must literally build word pictures out of the facts.

Be conversational. The closer you get to normal speech patterns, the more believable you are. The reaction is... somebody out there is just standing and talking to me. Rather than... this is another commercial.

Pin-point your audience. In merchandise and approach. If your radio station tells you that, in your time slots, you'll be reaching a young audience . . . don't try to sell them good but dumb fashions. And don't talk about what to wear when they drive the kids to school. Suit the commercial to your audience. It pays off.

Humor seems to work on radio. It's very hard to be funny . . . and sell . . . in print. But somehow you can be completely whacky on the air . . . successfully. Try it, if it's your thing.

If you're lucky enough to have two voices, try to develop a little plot. Conflict . . . like a novel. Pit the smart one against the stupid one, generation against generation, men against women. Polarization? Sure, but all in fun!

Always end upbeat. Not with just your address. Add a short phrase or word, Maybe one that you can repeat in all your commercials. *Worth seeing. Not to be missed. Waiting for you now. Remarkable. You'll love what you find.*

Some things to avoid

The worst possible radio ad is a laundry list. 5 items with 10 prices. You merely confuse the listener.

If your merchants don't understand this, demonstrate it. Prepare a commercial with 5 items unfamiliar to them, then one hour later test them to see how much they remember. You'll never get a laundry list again!

Price ranges are almost as bad. In an ad, you can have a listing that explains the range. But when you say $19 to $190 on the air, you've not told the customer what she can expect to pay when she comes dashing in. So she won't.

Don't list a half dozen stores with their addresses. If you have that many. Just "At all the stores". Either they'll know them. Or look them up in the phone book.

Stay away from mood music. "For the woman who raises Dalmatians and wears a nest of robins in her hair". Talk about the merchandise. Your listener knows who she is. Leave the precious prose to the cosmetic people. They need it. They have nothing to say. Exception: when you have merchandise that could be either male or female, don't leave them in doubt. Say "misses sizes". Or something to clue the audience in. Fast.

A word about jingles. No. Jingles are hard to understand, since they are rarely well articulated. They waste words. You always do when you have to rhyme. True, they give you identification, but they don't give you the room to sell. Now, music . . . that's something else.

Music

A few notes of the right music, at the beginning of a commercial . . . and maybe at the end, will give you quick identification on the air. Your theme song.

Where do you get the music? The expensive way is to have special music composed and recorded. National manufacturers do this. The inexpensive way is to ask your radio station. You'll find that most stations "own" bits of music. They'll send you tapes. Listen, then choose the piece you want. Ask them to reserve it for you exclusively; presto . . . you've got yourself a theme.

Scheduling radio ads

A few spots spaced out over a week will do you no good at all. Radio time should be bought in "flights" . . . concentrated periods of time. If you can afford only 10 spots, run them in one day or save the money for your newspaper ads.

When should you be on the air? Let the experts at the radio station help you. They know who's listening at what hour and can give you the audience you want. Wide or narrow.

The 30-second versus the one-minute

In some areas, minutes cost only a few bucks more than 30-second spots. However. It's difficult to keep audience interest for a whole minute. Unless you use two voices. It can be done, but it takes tremendous skill. Besides which, if you buy 30's, you can spread them and reach a larger audience.

If minutes are an irresistible buy, you're better off breaking your minutes into two 30-second segments and doing 2 complete and separate ads. (This is known as two 30's back-to-back.) Why not just take the minute and do two items? It's simpler . . . and more memorable . . . to sell each item separately. You don't need a common denominator. You can run disparate items. You won't bore your listeners with a whole minute.

Lest we sound down on one-minute spots let us assure you that there are times when they work. And work well. When you're on tape and have two voices to play with. When you have a real news story. What's happening at your store for Christmas. A storewide sale. A new department. A special event. A vast assortment. You'll notice that these are more or less institutional in nature. With the possible exception of the special event, try to include a specific item at a price in these messages. Then you can check the effectiveness of your commercial. When you use a minute, you have plenty of time.

What if you have a merchandise story so complex that you can't do it in the 75 words of a 30-second spot? Should you take a minute to tell it? No. Either simplify your story . . . or don't use radio for it.

Live verses tape

An announcer reading your commercial "live" has an immediacy, an urgency. It becomes news. It also has flexibility. Want to change it? Just zip a new commercial down to the station.

BUT. You can only use the announcers' voices. Voices that may be used by a half-dozen other companies in the area. Voices that vary, depending on the time you're on the air. Also, there are no rehearsals. No play through to hear how it sounds . . . to fuss over and make small emphasis changes.

It costs so little to tape these days that it's a shame not to do it. You get professionalism, a consistency you can't get live. You can use music and sound effects. You can use two or more voices. You can be distinctive. Which means identification. Which, when you have no logo to display, is so important.

Suggested copy

If a personality or a D.J. is going to deliver your message, you may be asked for a list of facts or suggested copy instead of a formal commercial. Be absolutely sure that you list facts in order of importance (and that this is clearly understood.) Otherwise you may end up with a long burble about the print on a scarf, and no mention of the fact that it is hand-rolled pure silk.

How much merchandise and which

Since radio has no pictures, you must choose merchandise that is communicable in words. A few words. You'd be surprised how fast they get used up describing even the simplest fashion.

The 10-second ID is not suitable for most merchandise. Except a single item that needs no description at all. Famous-make panty hose. A collection of sweaters at a single price. A sale of handbags at a price. And their like. Obviously, you can't give colors or sizes or even facts in 25 words.

The best use of the ID is to announce an event. A post-Easter sale. A personal appearance by a celebrity. A service like free gift wrap. Just as a reminder to listeners.

A 30-second spot is best used for one or two items, preferably related ones. A skirt and shirt, for example. A group of items at a single price is workable, but don't merely list them. Use the "from . . . to" technique.

The minute? There are no rules. We once did a commercial with 26 items! That's right. It was an alphabetical listing of different kinds of pillows and started with abstract art pillows and ended with zebra-striped ones. We explained the gimmick, of course.

Since it's a problem to keep the audience listening, the technique of the one minute commercial is special. You just get yourself an idea and fly.

Note: This should be apparent, but we'll point it out anyway. There is no place on radio for also-rans. If you have 4 styles of suede jackets, you can only promote one . . . and mention the fact that there are others, without describing or pricing them.

CHAPTER 19.

TELEVISION

The subtitle for this chapter should have been: who's afraid of the big bad tube?

A lot of specialty stores are. Because they assume it's too expensive. Because it's unfamiliar and they're not sure how to handle it. Even because other stores in the area don't use TV, so they think .. if it's not for them, it's not for us.

But TV doesn't have to be all that expensive. And you don't have to .. in fact, you shouldn't .. create your own commercials. This is the time to use outside experts. Even the giant stores do.

How much does TV cost?

This divides itself into two parts: time cost and production costs.

If you're in a large city, like New York, Chicago, or L.A., TV time can be almost prohibitive. Since rates are based on number of viewers. However, there are often bargains to be had. How can you find out about them? From the TV station or the media buyer of an ad agency.

Once you get into the smaller cities, the cost of TV time drops and drops and drops. It can be a very attractive buy. Don't be afraid to ask about rates. You commit yourself to nothing.

Production costs can run into tens of thousands of dollars, or just a few hundred. To keep costs down, remember this:

1. You're not General Motors or the Green Giant. You don't have to compete with them. You're a familiar name to most of the viewers.

2. TV is not show biz. You don't have to produce a 30-second drama to get attention. What you have to say and show is news to your customers and should be presented as news. Straight. Without a plot. Without all the theatrical trimmings.

135

3. Many TV studios will take color shots for you at a couple of bucks each. They'll take them out on location and can catch, in a still, much of the motion and excitement and mood you want.

4. It's possible to buy "canned" TV commercials for under a hundred bucks. If it's the merchandise you want to promote, you're in clover.

5. Unlike newspaper ads, a TV commercial can be used many times over. When you figure production costs, they should be amortized for the life of the commercial.

6. An interesting way to save money is the "doughnut" technique. You create a standard opening and closing, as beautifully done as you can afford, with music .. the works. Then you slip a merchandise segment into the "hole". This gives you flexibility; you can keep changing the "hole". It gives you the identification of a constant opening and closing. Most importantly, since you only have to produce the "hole" each time, each commercial costs less. Be sure, however, that your opening and closing are broad enough to cover all bases. Either a superiority, a season, or pin-pointing an audience.

Think how nicely this can work, for example, at Christmas, Or Spring. Or to reach a special audience.

Incidentally, you can do the same thing on radio. It's a bit trickier because there's no visual, but no less effective if well done.

Who should buy TV time?

TV, like radio, is sold as 10-second ID's, 30 seconds and minutes. Sometimes you can also buy 20-second spots. Since even the fattest corporations have stopped using minutes, you might as well forget them, too.

You can, of course, negotiate your TV buy directly. However, if you plan to use an agency to produce your TV, let them do the bargaining. They have more clout. They buy TV for any number of clients. They usually can get you better time slots and, often as not, a better price.

136

Here again, don't expect 3 commercials spread out over a week to create much of an impression. Concentrate your effort intensively. What's known as vertical saturation. Many times during the day. Hit hard, then get off the tube.

Who should produce TV?

TV is a special medium, demanding special techniques. Unless your background is TV, leave it to the experts. That means an ad agency, a TV production company, or your TV station. If they offer that kind of service. Make a friend of the TV director at any of these places. He'll share his know-how and you may even get to be an expert yourself.

The script, however, should either come out of your advertising department or be worked out with you. Even if you've never written a script before, you know more about your store and its merchandise than a stranger.

Note: Always be present when a TV commercial is shot. TV directors are not merchants. They're just as likely to concentrate on a pretty face as on the details of a garment. Which is not what you're selling.

The TV commercial

The main thing to keep in mind is that TV is action, motion. It involves the viewer in a demonstration ... not a description. Which is one reason why it's so effective for fashion. Yet it still must do what any other ad does. Your commercial must give customer benefits, it must sell, it must provide facts, emphasize your superiority, and urge the viewer to action. All in as few words as possible!

Every commercial consists of 3 parts. The video (the pictures), the audio (the spoken words) and the supers (the words superimposed on the screen).

The video: You can use slides. They're cheap, but unless carefully done, they can look cheap. Or you can use film or tape.

Action! You'll have to decide whether it's worth the difference in cost. We've seen great commercials in both techniques. And bad ones, too.

The audio: Most retail stores use "voice over", an announcer talking while the pictures are showing. This saves money and production time. Also it's easier to find good actors or models and good voices in separate bodies. They so rarely seem to come in one package.

The super: The fewer of these the better. They can add a lot of emphasis. Especially when the words on the screen are the same as the words the announcer is saying. But they can also be very distracting. They are especially good for numbers ... prices, addresses, phone number. Most people have visual rather than oral memories.

You must maintain a balance between video, audio, and supers. You simply can't have all 3 going at once all the time. The viewer can't concentrate on a glorious blazer if you're talking about the fabric and the super is listing colors .. all at once.

There must also be breathing time. When only the picture is showing ... without words. This is like white space in an ad. Even more important on TV, because TV moves so fast, has so much going on.

The merchandise

TV is action. As we keep saying. You need merchandise that is graphic and moves well. Ideally, you shouldn't think in terms of showing a dress, but a person moving around in it. Anything from coming through a door to lighting candles. Your buyers will be glad to hear that this is one time we never say no when they ask for a back view or a close-up of details. They work beautifully on TV.

Warning: TV shows it like it is. You can't retouch film or tape, at least not economically. Your picture is not interpreted, screened through an artist's eyes. That means no faking. Clothes must be provided in correct size .. and fitted precisely. Accessories must

138

be perfect. You're selling a total impression, not just a garment. That's why you shouldn't depend on the TV producer to provide anything, not even a pair of pantyhose or earrings. You should control everything that's seen on the screen, even if it's seen only for a moment.

The camera can do funny things to color. And most TV is now in full color. Before you decide on a color for merchandise and accessories, ask the TV experts how it will look. Or give them a choice of colors and let them tell you which.

How much merchandise?

You may think that, because you're showing the goods and consequently don't need as many words to describe it, you can jam a TV commercial.

This is not true. The viewer can't replay your commercial. Once the merchandise is off the screen, it's gone. Forever. A quick glimpse is not enough to sell from. The desire to buy must be built slowly.

The ideal for a 30-second spot is one item. Handled lovingly, in depth and detail. But who can always afford it?

The alternative is a group of merchandise with a common denominator. A group of pant coats. Boots at a single price. Or a single fashion story .. feathers or a color or whatever. Then you can use 3, possibly 4, pieces of merchandise if the group has both a single idea and a single price.

If you have a broad news or fashion story to tell, you can show more. But don't expect to sell the individual items. All you can sell is the idea, and your store as the place to find it.

The script

Every principle of writing good copy applies. Plus the use of special techniques. Here are some do's and don'ts.

1. *Do pare your facts down to the essentials.* Let the video tell as much of the story as you can. Use words only for emphasis, to

139

give the customer benefits, point out the fashion news, and provide information that the picture can't provide.

This takes a turnaround in thinking. To give a simple example: if you ran an all-weather coat in the papers, you'd probably say something about how it takes to rain or shine. Your TV video can show both the rainstorm and the sunshine. You don't need words. Or "Men's Shirts". You'll show men.

2. *Do give enough facts to turn the viewer into a buyer.* That means colors, sizes, fabrics, price. Much of this can be "supered", but it must be there.

3. *Don't get yourself involved in so much story or plot or the sheer glamor of TV that it's hard to tell what you're selling.* Stick with the merchandise and let your script spring from it.

4. *Do be brief, conversational.* Use incomplete sentences, and banish clauses. That's the way most people talk.

5. *Do be sure it's absolutely clear that this is your store's TV commercial.* It should reflect your store's personality. And don't be afraid to keep using your name. Not only as a sign-off, but during the commercial.

6. *Do end with an urge to action.* That's why you're on the tube. To get business.

7. *If you're writing for slides,* don't write so many words for any one slide that it just sits there. And sits. That's not TV.

8. *Finally ... don't forget to ask your TV station who your audience is ..* and write to them. Your audience may be just People. OK, write to people, but not to an abstraction. A sound approach for any medium.

No matter how good a writer you are, it's impossible to write only the audio, and let someone else dream up the video afterwards. TV is a true marriage of pictures and words. You must do both audio and video (even if it's only a suggested video) yourself. Or work closely with the person doing the video. And by closely, we mean side by side. On the other hand, you can fit words to existing video. That's because TV is a picture medium with words.

Lead time

Don't be surprised if you're told that it takes 4 to 6 weeks to produce your commercial. Especially if it's going to be shot on location. It's possible to produce a TV spot in a couple of days. In an emergency. But it's better to give the producer the time he requests. You'll get a superior product most of the time.

Changes

One your commercial is in the can, the cost of changing it is exorbitant. On film or slides. On tape, it's almost impossible. So make your changes on the script, the storyboard, or even while the commercial is being produced.

Impress this on your buyers and get their changes before you go into production. Double-check every fact, and the stock situation. And keep checking up to the minute you're in front of the camera. If your buyers (like all too many) are accustomed to changing prices or colors when the merchandise finally arrives .. or on proof... you may be in for big trouble and expense.

The ready-made commercial

Many stores buy TV spots from companies that produce them and sell the same commercials to lots of stores. This brings the price down for each store. If it's the merchandise you want to advertise, this is a good buy. You'll have far better production than you can afford. These companies work with resources, use top talent, and often film in far-off places. The video is almost always superb. But the audio MUST be changed. Since it's usually voice-over, this is no problem. All you need do is write a new script to the video and tape it. Why bother? Because these commercials go to many stores, they're general. Too general to do a good selling job for you. You must use your own words, talk to your own customers, sell your own store. Personally. The canned commercial can't do this. Only you can.

The vendor commercial
One of your resources buys a flight of spots on your TV station. Since he'd like to see some immediate results, he comes to you and offers to put "Available at XX store"at the end.

Should you accept? Only if it's merchandise you have in stock .. and don't have to go out and buy. Only if it's merchandise you'd like to expose because it's timely, characteristic of your store, right for your audience. Only if he lets you look at the commercial, or the storyboard, in advance. To make sure he's not violating store policy. Or making a competitive statement that will enrage your other resources.

If his commercial meets all these criteria .. why not? It doesn't cost you anything. And might bring you business. And your name to a new audience.

Some vendors supply excellent slides and "wild footage" of their products. These can be incorporated into commercials that come across with your personality and individuality. If you buy TV time, ask your key suppliers what TV aids they have.

Is TV for you?
Try a sale. It's the easiest way to get results quickly. But give it a fair try. Take enough spots to make an impression. And confine the sale to TV. Then check the results.

CHAPTER 20.

ESPECIALLY FOR YOU

This is a miscellany of situations, quandries, and questions that arise primarily in smaller stores. Some happen because you're trying to make each dollar work like three (although the best way to do this is still to create better ads!). Some are inherent in being small and a small advertiser. Some are due to lack of knowledge or bad lines of communication.

As we said: a miscellany. Not in any order of importance.

"Similar" merchandise

You're trying to save money on art. Or you can't find an artist. Or you have an ad ready to release, but the merchandise is still on the loading platform and there's no time to do the artwork. So you go through manufacturer's mats, stuff from your buying office, and "Women's Wear". You spot something that looks like what you're selling .. and put that into your ad. Since your conscience bothers you, you add a line at the bottom "Similar to picture shown".

Don't. Don't. Don't.

You're better off, about a thousand times over, with an all type ad. Anything that might possibly be misinterpreted or mislead the customer is bad business. Suppose your "similar" merchandise has long sleeves, and the art you swipe has short. Suppose Miss Q only wants short sleeves. Suppose she spends 2 gallons of gas and an hour or so to get to you and back. Only to be disappointed. Do you think you've made a customer?

To put it in other terms. Imagine a restaurant listing steak on its menu and saying their specialty is similar. Pot roast!

We know the rationalization. If she doesn't like what we advertised, we'll sell her something else. Not these days. Customers know what they want. It's too risky.

143

Note: There's nothing wrong with using swipes. As a starter, for the figure, the position. Then trace it, changing every detail so it becomes a picture of your goods. Literally, exactly, precisely what you're selling.

Price ranges

Because small stores can't afford the space for a separate ad on each item, their ads are often pocked with price ranges. This is unavoidable. But there's a right way and a wrong way to use these price ranges.

If you're showing six shirts at six different prices and you want a big price impression, you can say "$19 to $33". Provided you then spell out the price of each shirt. You can have a list of one-line descriptions of the shirts, each ending in a price. You can put a small price next to each shirt. Which, admittedly, can mess up the art. You can key the art and the prices. (A $22. B. $19. Etc.). It's vital that the customer know the price of the shirt she's interested in. Even if you want her to come see rather than order by phone or by mail.

In some areas, it's illegal to make indefinite statements like "priced from $17" or "save up to 50%". Legal or not, you shouldn't. It smacks of chicanery. Leave that kind of trick to fly-by-nights.

As we told you in the Sale Chapter, when you use percentages, always do the arithmetic for the customer. We see this sort of thing repeatedly. "25% off all shoes, reg. $21 to $39". What's wrong? The customer glancing at your ad will think the selling price is $21 to $39. You must also tell her what she'll pay. You must say "now 13.75 to 29.95". Don't be afraid of a lot of numbers ... when they make sense. Just design them nicely and clearly. And do the arithmetic even when it's easy .. like half price. So no misinterpretation is possible.

If you use ranges, either price or percentage, on sales, be fair to . the customer. Have enough stock of the highest and the lowest. So if she turns up reasonably early, she'll find it in stock. Or else spell out quantities. Just 4 pairs of plaid pants, reg. $45, now $15.

Some specialty stores seem to think that the dollar sign is vulgar. If it's not good enough for Cartier, it's not good enough for them. So they end up with "Panties, 4 for 5". Not only silly, but confusing. Or they spell everything out. "Coats, $98.00". Which, psychologically, makes the price look higher. The accepted practice (translation: what the reader is accustomed to and understands immediately) is this. When there are no pennies, use $5 or 5.00. When there are pennies, use the decimal point 5.50. Over $100, skip the .00 ($137).

Re-using old art

A few caveats here. Use it only if it's identical merchandise. Only if you've looked it over carefully and the accessories are still seasonal and right. If it's being used with other merchandise, only if it's in the same style (preferably by the same artist) and in proper scale. Otherwise you'll end up with a patchwork that spoils the impression you've tried so hard to make.

Borders

This is an often-used device for quick recognition in the papers. And for keeping other ads from crowding too closely on yours.

Your newspaper or typographic house has an almost endless number of stock borders. Or you can put one together from standard items. Or you can have one hand-drawn.

If you decide to use a border, first be sure that no other store in the paper is using the same one. Be sure it's in character with your type style, your art work, and the character of your ads and your store. Be sure that, if you blow it up for a larger ad, it doesn't look clumsy or so dark it dominates the ad.

Always design your ad inside the border. Don't tack it on after the ad is finished. As a strong graphic element, it has to relate to your other graphics.

Note: Before you decide you need a border, ask yourself whether a little more white space around your ad wouldn't do the job.

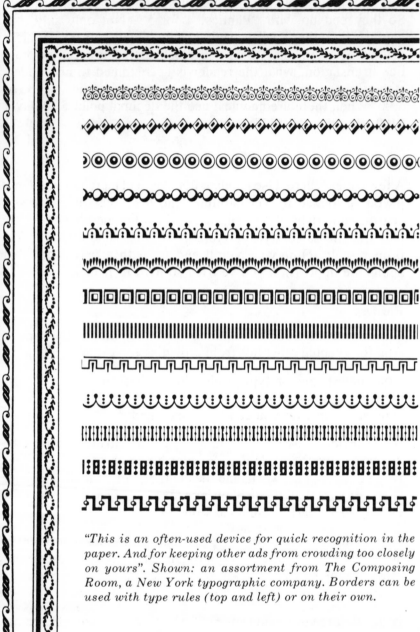

"This is an often-used device for quick recognition in the paper. And for keeping other ads from crowding too closely on yours". Shown: an assortment from The Composing Room, a New York typographic company. Borders can be used with type rules (top and left) or on their own.

Campaigns

Is it possible to have a campaign when you're in the newspapers only a couple of times a week? Do you need it?

If you're asking questions like this, you probably don't understand the nature of a campaign. Which is two-fold.

What most of us think of as a campaign is 6 ads in 3 days on pink for Spring. Or a British Fortnight with dozens of ads in 2 weeks. Or when a store latches on to an idea like "Women on Wheels" and runs with it.

Obviously not for the small store.

But there are other kinds of campaigns. Some of which you're probably running right now. Only you don't think of them as such. Your whole Christmas effort is .. or should be .. a campaign. Mother's Day. Father's Day. Back to School and Work. Your "young" departments. Your boutique or salon-type department.

What makes these campaigns? Pre-planning. So certain elements are repeated, ad after ad. This can be graphics ... variations on a layout (which is dramatically different from your day-in-day-out layout). It can be the style and the way you use type. It can be language and copy. Saks 5th Avenue, for example, built all their Christmas 1975 advertising around the phrase "I Love It". With first person copy. In newspapers, in magazines. The common denominator was the phrase and the copy approach.

The small store's chief problem is that it must keep a concept going longer to make a real impression. 3 ads do not a campaign make!

That means your campaign idea must be broad enough to fit all your advertising for a period of time. And merchandised to it. This cannot be done as the ads come on schedule. It must be pre-planned as a whole.

We mentioned Christmas campaigns. They're easy. Strew a couple of stars or snow-flakes or sprigs of holly around any ad. Run it after Thanksgiving and it says Christmas.

147

You should try to be as simple and direct with other campaign ideas. Naturally, this is in direct ratio to the amount of advertising you do. A complex idea takes more ads to get across.

For example:
You're a men's store and your total Father's Day effort is 4 ads in the week before the event. Run straight advertising and make it a campaign with a phrase about Father or his Day.

For Mother's Day, a small fashion store can sprout a couple of carnations from the logo or the headline. And, again, say something nice about mother. Nothing elaborate. Nothing that takes a lot of time or money or space.

These are merchandise campaigns. The merchandise is the most important element. It should dominate the ad. Don't waste space or time on gimmicks.

How about institutional campaigns? Yes, you can afford them. We have a favorite device that we know works equally well for Macy's New York, the world's largest store, and one of our clients with an annual volume of 1 million (but growing!) Move the logotype to the left of your ad. Then take the equivalent depth on the right side (or vice versa) for a couple of lines. Interesting, sprightly lines with a bold-face lead-in or little heading that's provocative. It's the best at the top of your ad, but will also get itself read at the bottom. No extra linage, and a chance to tell the stories you never seem to tell. From gift wraps to assortments to fashion news.

Must you use the same campaign in all media? Only if you're talking to the same people. If you use a lot of radio to reach young people, this can be a campaign on its own. Unrelated to what you're doing in the newspaper. But watch out. Or you'll be fragmenting your advertising impression.

Vendor money

We are often asked how to get vendor money for ads. You ask. Buyers should be instructed to ask, routinely, every time they're in the market. All that can happen is that they'll be turned down.

If you remember our chapter on vendor-paid advertising, the trick is to get money with the fewest possible strings attached. Then handle it as tenderly as though it were your own money. To create great ads. (Just be sure to follow FTC Guides on Promotional Allowances.)

Lease department advertising

Your lease departments may be delighted to be part of your regular advertising. No problem.

On the other hand, they may present you with mats or mechanicals and say … this is what you must run. Especially if they belong to a big national chain.

Like vendor ads, the only ones who should know it's lease department advertising are you and your lessee. You are one store. And should be talking to the customer from one point of view. By adding their dollars to yours this way, you will both benefit by broader impact.

Chances are that the ad people turning out mats for your leased shoe operation or furs or photo studio or beauty salon or you-name-it, have never been in your store. Or your town. And certainly not seen your ads.

If their ads are wrong for you, it's not really their fault. It's yours. For running them. Because it's easier, it's cheaper, it's less hassle than asserting your right to your own advertising.

Persuading them to let you do ads your own way may take some delicate dialogue.

But you must try. And try.

What if they insist on their own ads? Which are out of character with yours? Start with the compromise ploy. You'll use their art, but write your own copy. If this won't work (and more often than not, it will), you have no choice. Don't incorporate their ads into yours. Run them alongside or even on a different page. Don't sacrifice the impression you are making. Including their ads may

149

make your own ads bigger. But what you want are better ads, not necessarily bigger ones.

Exclusive items

When an item belongs just to you in the area, shout, boast, emphasize this fact. It's the best possible reason for shopping at your store: the customer can't get it somewhere else.

Makes sense? Of course. So what do you see in the newspaper? Some bit of fluff about the merchandise, and a line at the end of the copy "ours exclusively". Is this the way to treat one of your strongest selling points?

Why does this happen? Writers think this approach is uncreative. Designers hate another element in their pretty layouts. If you don't want another element, build the exclusive story into your headline. Or subhead. Or start your copy with it .. and underline or italicize it. Or, if you display a price, put it alongside the price.

Just don't bury it or handle it as an after-thought. In our mass-produced, mechanized, homogenized world, "ours alone" or "exclusively ours" makes the merchandise sound like a limited edition. Currently a desirable quality.

Out-thinking the competiton

Off-beat scheduling is one way. Discussed in Chapter 4. Another is the timing of your events.

If every store in town starts its clearances the day after Christmas, start yours the week before. After-Christmas prices before Christmas. Many stores are doing this . . . with huge results.

Do Fall fashions break in your newspaper in August? When customers are still sweating it out in little cottons? Save your big money for the big spending time in September, then hit hard.

These are elementary examples. Cited so you can see the potential in re-examining when you run every event. Not because that's when you've always run it. Not because that's when "they" run it. But because the timing is faultless. Or because you can throw your competition off-balance. (Naturally, you'll have to go through the re-examination process every year. They're not dumb. They'll anticipate you next year.)

Often off-beat position in the paper can bring unexpected results. It's still another way to out-think the competition.

In one town, the supermarkets started to take 7 columns instead of full pages on "food day". Normally, specialty stores were out of the paper that day on the theory that customers were shopping for franks, not finery. One store, however, developed a half-page one column format to run alongside the most popular supermarket's ad. It pulled fantastically. Why? With food prices the way they are, supermarket specials get tremendous readership. So did the little ad.

This was deliberate, and smart reasoning. It can also happen by accident. A fine domestics store, near a cluster of retirement communities in Florida, advertised bridge table covers. The newspaper ran the ad on the obituary page. Orders poured in. Aha, said the owner, I've got me a hot item. He repeated the ad. Which then ran in the regular part of the newspaper. Normal response. What happened, of course, is that retired people read obituaries. They saw his ad there, but missed it in the more competitive market place up front.

Look at your own newspaper .. and see. Maybe there's some page, some day, some section where competition doesn't advertise. That might pull for you. There are some obvious ones that are usually good bets. Perfume and gift certificates before Christmas or Mother's Day in the financial pages. Active sport clothes in the sporting pages (yes, women do read the sports news). Even at-home fashions facing the TV listings.

What should you do when your competition opens a new store or department or launches a spectacular or their biggest sale ever or celebrates a 50th birthday? Nothing. Let them have their day, instead of crippling your budget by trying to compete. Then, when they run out of steam and dollars, do your damndest.

Possible exception. If it is their 50th or 75th or some other significant birthday, a small ad or paragraph in your ad congratulating them (as wittily as possible) will earn you lots of pleasant comments around town.

Adding a little something at the last minute

The copy is written. The layout finished. The artwork delivered. You are proudly showing the whole package to the boss. Who says .. can't we squeeze in a paragraph about our January coat sale that's still going on?

Sound familiar? Let's add the buyer who suddenly gets a deal on chokers and wants to throw them into his Sunday ad. With 3 illustrations, natch.

If you can't talk them out of it (you should try), the wrong thing to do is literally squeeze or throw them in. You must go back to the layout pad and redesign the ad. Sorry. An ad is a totality. You can't graft another element into it, or subtract (this happens too ... "just spread it out" they say, when the cerise sneakers in the feature box don't arrive on time).

Most merchants don't realize this. We haven't told them. You'll do yourself a favor if you do. Pointing out how much time it takes to incorporate another "little" thing into an ad at this stage. Point it out every time and maybe they'll get the message.

Proofs and corrections

If your buyers see manuscript and layout, there should be no need to make changes on proof. Barring an occasional price or color or size change. Because the goods came in late. And different.

Some stores don't even show proof to buyers.

Whether they're correcting manuscript or proofs, life will be easier (and errors fewer) if you insist on certain rules. And get management to back you up. Firmly.

1. No writing between the lines. If they change copy or add to it, they must draw a line out to the margin, make a circle, and write the change inside the circle.

2. If they make drastic changes (concept, amount of copy or headline, art,) they must bring those changes, in person, into the advertising department.

3. Changes cost money once the ad is on proof. The more accurate their information sheets, the fewer changes. They must understand there's no such thing as a small change. If they told you the baby snowsuit came in pink and blue and it turns out to be aquamarine, marigold, and watermelon, a whole paragraph may need resetting. Even when big changes are made on manuscript, this takes time. And time is money.

4. You'll find a list of frequently used proof-readers' marks in the Appendix. Xerox it or make up your own list and give it to your buyers. Urge them to use these marks. So you'll all be talking the same language.

Tip: When you check proofs against manuscript, get someone to read the manuscript aloud to you. It's almost impossible to proof-read what you've written yourself. You know what it should be, so your eye sees it that way.

The boss who's always on your back

You know, he thinks he's an ad whiz. He goes off on vacation and sends back clippings. He thumbs through the New York Times and tosses a 7 column ad at you and asks .. why don't we do that .. a lot smaller, of course? He clips the competition's ad and says .. next time we have belts, this is the ad I want.

What do you do? Besides quit?

Make him part of the team. Get him involved in why you're doing an ad the way you are. Discuss ads and ideas with him. He'll become part of the decision-making process. You'll have his OK in advance! And he won't have a surprise when he sees proof or opens his paper or tunes in his radio.

Best of all, if you can pile up a couple of successes doing ads the way you want to do them, he may end up minding his business instead of yours.

The real trouble is that advertising is "glamorous". They want to be part of it. Remember this, and maybe the situation will be more tolerable.

Tip: If you really want him on your side, we suggest our previous book, "The Secret Ingredient of Good Retail Ads: A Handbook for Buyers and their Bosses". He may still look over your shoulder, but at least he'll understand what you're trying to do.

CHAPTER 21.

HOW TO MEASURE
ADVERTISING RESULTS

A good ad executive is a good merchant.

Your stock in trade is your creativity. Plus your ability to translate the store's merchandise and philosophy into ads that move people to act.

You take pride in what you've done ... the store's ads in the newspaper. You influence people and enjoy watching them buy the goods you've advertised.

You always want to know .. how did the ad do?

That's what this chapter is all about.

Different ads are measured differently

There are lots of advertising ideas and lots of ways to present each of these ideas. No matter. Every ad should bring a measurable consumer response. If it doesn't, your ideas are wasted.

However, you should understand what to expect by way of response, depending on whether an ad puts its emphasis on volume, profit, or prestige.

Each category is subject to different modes of measurement.

Measuring the results of institutionals

As you know, this is advertising that creates and maintains the store's personality. It relates the store to the community, to contemporary events, to its services and personnel, to its merchandise superiorities and even to its pricing policy.

Institutional advertising can't be measured on the next day's or next week's sale sheet. Nor should it be.

How can Macy's measure the results of its Thanksgiving Day Parade ads? By counting the crowds that line the parade route? Or the millions watching on TV? Certainly there's no immediate reaction at the cash register.

Institutional advertising can really only be measured in decades. By the respect felt by customers and suppliers. By the way a store grows. And thrives. And profits.

Indirect advertising

This is the bulk of advertising for most specialty shops. It's advertising that creates and maintains the store's reputation .. through its merchandise.That's new, now or exclusive. That exposes superior assortments, superior quality, or superior design. Merchandise that has consumer demand.

Indirect advertising should bring an immediate response. However, final results should be tallied over a period of a week, a month, or a season. Not the next day.

The usual method is plus-over-normal. If the coat department would normally do $3000 that week ... and it does $4500 ... you can safely assume that the extra $1500 is due to the ad that ran.

With this big exception. There's a visible relationship between how much your customers want the goods and the speed with which they respond. Boots on a snowy day, advertised at regular prices, will bring them in. A new skirt length or a new fashion idea will be slower. Lots slower.

Direct advertising

Clearances, storewide and departmental sales, special purchases, regular merchandise with smaller than normal mark-ons to meet competition. That's direct advertising. Off-price. Reflecting the price and value policy of the store. Either planned or purely opportunistic.

Direct advertising should bring an immediate response.

This can be measured by the plus-over-normal method described above. Or the ratio of cost of ad to what it brings in. Many large stores use a 10 to 1 ratio. If the ad cost is $1000, the response should be $10,000. Less and it's not a success. More ... and you've got a winner.

Specialty stores , on the other hand, often find a 6-8 to 1 ratio more realistic. An ad costing $200 should bring in $1200 to $1600.

Why the difference between the large store and its smaller sisters? Traffic. Customers who buy the goods merely because they're there, exposed to it because they see it when they're shopping. And who may not have seen the ad.

The importance of measuring advertising results

The most frustrating answers you can get when you ask about the results of an ad are:

Lousy.

Fair.

Great!

We sold out.

I haven't had time to check.

You can probably add a few more. All generalities. Let's look at them, one by one, and translate them.

Lousy. A decisive, if hardly business-like, expletive that explains nothing. It gives the ad executive no basis for judging or re-examining the ad. Did it do no business at all? Didn't it attract a single customer? It's almost inconceivable that an ad, especially a direct ad, even a weak one, would have no measurable result. How can you review an ad with this kind of no-fact answer?

Fair. That's better. Somebody did come in and buy. But still a generality. How many were sold? Which styles? Which colors? Which sizes?

Answers to these questions would help decide the merchandise approach for future ads. Besides which, you need this information for re-orders.

Great! Happy day. He did business on the ad. Can he get more goods? How soon? Should the ad be repeated? A successful ad should be run again as soon as possible. As often as possible. Play the winners.

We sold out. Hurrah! Every one sold? Every color? Every size? Sorry .. he simply did not buy enough to support the ad.

Before the ad is released, the amount of stock to back it up should be reviewed ... and should be adequate. It's possible to go to press with a limited stock ... plus a firm promise for quick additional delivery from the manufacturer. But it's a gamble you shouldn't take too often.

I haven't had time to check. The great let-down. What could possibly be more important than knowing what customers are buying. Or not buying?

Knowing quickly what customers are buying is one of the most vital pieces of information to a specialty store. And what better way to find out <u>quickly</u> than through advertising results?

The computer breakdown you get at the end of every month is a great control and information device for the total store picture. If you have a computer. Even if you do have, the information is after the fact and hardly timely. The retail fashion business is too volatile for this. By the end of the month, your customers may be out of pink and into green. Your advertising results, however, are immediate. They show merchandise trends ... on the spot.

What can your advertising results show you ... quickly?

Whether your merchandise decision was right or wrong.

Whether you should repeat the ad or continue to stock the same colors, styles, and classifications. Or change.

Whether your ad techniques are pulling. Or not.

Which facts should your ad results state?

How much did the ad cost?

How much business did it bring in the first day, the second day, the week?

Which styles, colors, sizes sold best?

What business did the department do?

What was the total store business?

And let's not forget this: what was the weather?

Here's how to measure results

1. Check your stubs or sales slips or take an inventory count of the advertised merchandise at the end of the business day.

2. Each merchant should keep his own ad book (or the boss may keep it for all of them if the amount of advertising is small). Next to each ad, note: the number of units sold; comments on colors, styles and sizes sold; total department volume this year and the same day last year.

3. The ad department should have the identical material in its own ad book.

4. The information should be reviewed as quickly as possible by top management, advertising executive, and department manager. For conclusions and action.

Do this quickly, consistently, conscientiously ... and you'll know where you're going. You'll have a guide. To future advertising. To merchandising that advertising. There is no other way.

CHAPTER 22.

CHECKLIST:
HOW TO JUDGE YOUR ADVERTISING

We certainly don't believe that you can create good advertising by checking off a list. There are too many exceptions. Which is where creativity comes in. However, certain things are so obvious, ad after ad, commercial after commercial, that you should watch for them. So use these lists not as a guide, but a constant reminder. (The copy and graphics checklists are adapted from our book, "The Secret Ingredient of Good Retail Ads: A Handbook for Buyers and their Bosses".)

HOW TO JUDGE YOUR COPY

Does your headline give the news ... or is it merely a label? Think of the difference between "Forecast: a white winter", and "White winter coats". The picture will show coats, won't it?

Does your copy give the customer benefits .. or is it self-serving? Think of the difference between "save plenty" and "prices cut". Does it answer the question, "What will it do for me?"

Does your ad talk YOU ... rather than US or THEY?

Does your ad give a reason for buying ... or does it merely catalogue facts? Bullet copy has its place, but it's not the best way to sell. You can't create emotion in bullet copy.

Does your ad give a reason for buying at *your* **store?** Don't send them to the competition!

Does your ad end with a note of urgency .. or does it just sit there?

Is your ad topical or timely ...or so bland it slides past the reader? If you could have written the same ad in the same language last year ... where have you been?

160

Is the language fresh, upbeat, interesting ... or is it cliche-filled and plain dull?

Are your sentences short and fascinating ... or so involved that you lose your reader?

Does your ad include all the necessary facts ... or are you making it hard for the customer to shop? The little bugs at the bottom of the ad may be a nuisance to you, but may help the customer.

Does the ad involve your customers ... talk to them in their own language, their own frame of reference? Do you know whom you're talking to?

Is your ad as specific as it can be made ... or is it so general that it says nothing?

Is your ad honest ... or full of poetic license?

Is your ad convincing ... or are you telling them WHAT, without telling them WHY?

Is the ad recognizable as your ad ... the language, the approach, the style? Or could it be anybody's ad?

Would it sell *you?*

HOW TO JUDGE YOUR GRAPHICS

Does the ad have a focal point ... or is everything so evenly spaced that there's nothing to grab your eye?

Is the art sharp and clear ... or a blurry gray mass?

Does the art look like your store and reflect your store's personality ... or is it out of character with everything you stand for?

Is the art in proper relationship to the copy ... or are you giving too much space to a long copy story when art could do the selling. Or wasting space on a big meaningless picture when words can do a better selling job?

161

Does the eye follow from element to element naturally ... or are there lots of irrelevant elements or gimmicks that stop the reader from reading?

Are your art and copy in the same sequence ... or are you asking the reader to hunt and pick?

Is your use of color meaningful to the merchandise ... or are you using color merely for the sake of color?

Is your store's logotype legible, easy to find, and consistent with store policy ... or does your ad look anonymous?

Are you trying to show too many things in one ad? Learn to say "no" to your merchants when the end result must be a poor ad.

Is everything so big that the reader can't see anything?

Is all merchandise clearly priced ... or are you making it hard for customers to know what they get for their money?

Is the art doing something for you ... or would you be better off with a dramatic all-type ad?

Are you using so many type styles and sizes that the reader's eye doesn't know what to look at first?

Can you read the ad ... even if you don't have 20-20 vision?

Would the ad bring _you_ into the store?

HOW TO JUDGE RADIO

All the principles of good copy apply: benefits, facts, news, honesty, et al. Plus a few special requirements of radio.

Is your name repeated often enough ... or won't they know where to go to get what you're advertising?

Do you have an intriguing lead-in ... or will they turn off their ears before you even begin your pitch?

Have you painted a vivid word picture ... so they can visualize what you're selling, even without a picture?

Do you have so many numbers they need a calculator to follow you? Remember... most people have visual rather than oral memories for numbers. Use only a few ... and repeat those.

Do you have quick identification ... music, voice, sound effects, tag lines?

Do you urge them to take action ... or does your commercial end in a dying fall?

Is your message nicely paced ... or are you cramming so many words into it that it's hard to listen to?

Is your commercial interesting? Would it make *you* listen?

HOW TO JUDGE TV

As we said above. All the principles of good advertising apply. Plus some special requirements.

Can they tell what you're selling ... or is it so wrapped in plot and fantasy that it's more entertainment than merchandise?

Can they tell it's *your* TV spot ... or are you assuming too much?

Does the merchandise look good? If it doesn't you should have saved your money.

Do the colors look right? Or have you chosen colors that tend to go "off"?

Do you give enough facts to turn the viewer into a customer ... or is it primarily mood music?

Does it give the viewer enough time to absorb what you're saying ... or is it a 3-ring circus?

Does it have action and motion? Otherwise, why go on TV?

Does it give the news ... look like news, sound like news? That's what they want from you!

Is it worth watching? Or will they raid the refrigerator on *your* time?

APPENDIX

FORMS

Here are 4 of the most commonly used forms, to use or to adapt to your store's particular need.

Always be sure to get a signature and phone extension on the ad request and sign information forms. They feel more responsible if they sign it!

Request for information for advertising

ADVERTISING REQUEST:

DATE AD WILL RUN _____ NEWSPAPER _____

BUYER _____ DEPT. _____ SIZE OF AD _____

IS MERCHANDISE EXCLUSIVE?   Yes ☐   No ☐

NUMBER OF SKETCHES: _____

IS MERCHANDISE IN STORE: _____

(If not, when will it arrive _____)

ITEM	STYLE NO.	PRICE	SIZES	COLORS	FABRICS

SELLING POINTS AND CUSTOMER BENEFITS. LIST IN ORDER OF IMPORTANCE. BE SPECIFIC _____

_____

_____

_____

_____

IS THIS A CO-OP AD? PLEASE GIVE FOLLOWING INFORMATION

MANUFACTURER _____   CO-OP AGREEMENT $_____

STREET ADDRESS _____   % _____

CITY _____ STATE _____ ZIP _____

IS MANUFACTURER'S LOGO OR SIG CUT NEEDED? Yes ☐   No ☐

MAIL ORDERS _____   PHONE ORDERS _____

LOCATIONS WHERE ADVERTISED MERCHANDISE WILL BE SOLD
(please circle)

STORE A   STORE B   STORE C   STORE D

ADVERTISING REQUESTS MUST BE FILLED OUT COMPLETELY AND MUST BE IN THE ADVERTISING DEPARTMENT NO LATER THAN 00 DAYS BEFORE THE AD DATE

Signature _____ Date _____

167

Request for sign

Dept. _____ Date sign required _____

Window # _____

Interior   (advertised) ☐   (not advertised) ☐

Item _____

Style #_____   Price _____   Comparative Price _____

Description: selling points in order of importance.

_____

_____

_____

Colors _____

Sizes _____

Fabric _____

Signature _____   Date _____

Special event plan

	date ready	person responsible
Name of event		
Date of event		
Window signs and posters		
Bill enclosure		
Press release		
Photographs for press release		
Contest box and blanks (or any other special equipment necessary)		
Newspaper advertising (schedule to be published)		
Radio commercials (schedule to be published)		

STORE NAME
STREET ADDRESS
CITY & STATE

Statement of Agreement for Cooperative Advertising

STORE NAME will advertise _____

_____OF:

_____

seller's name

_____

address

_____

city   state   zip

IN_____

(medium)

ON_____

date

THE SELLER hereby agrees to reimburse STORE NAME

_____

_____ for this service,

providing that the following requirements are met:

_____

_____

PAYMENT TO BE MADE UPON RECEIPT OF INVOICE and proof of peformance from STORE NAME

THE SELLER assures STORE NAME that this agreement is consistent with THE SELLER'S cooperative advertising allowance program, and that the SELLER'S plan has been affirmatively offered, and is otherwise available, on proportionately equal terms to all retailers competing with STORE NAME in the resale of the seller's products, including those retailers who purchase the SELLER'S products from wholesalers.

Date _____   _____

Authorized Seller's Representative

_____

Buyer for Store Name

Approved by:

_____

Store Name Advertising Director

The above form is similar to that used by one large department store. Note that this store precisely covers obligations under the Robinson Patman Act and Federal Trade Commission Guides.

169

Cooperative Advertising Agreement

Date_____, 1977

WITH (MANUFACTURER)_____

ADDRESS_____

CITY_____STATE_____ ZIP_____

agrees to provide a promotional/advertising allowance to_____
(store name)

_____ for promotion of_____

(merchandise _____

paying a total sum of $_____ or allowing_____% of store purchases.

MEDIA TO BE USED:	STORE RATE			TOTAL COST
NEWSPAPER_____	_____	Linage_____	$_____
TELEVISION_____	_____	Spots_____	$_____
RADIO_____	_____	Spots_____	$_____
CATALOG_____	_____	Space_____	$_____
DISPLAYS_____	_____	Type_____	$_____
OTHER_____	_____	Descrip. _____	$_____

(Fill in or check appropriate spaces.)

TIMING:_____

SPECIAL REQUIREMENTS FOR STORE OR SOURCE
(no verbal understandings):

I certify that the allowances given to_____ are in accordance with all
(store name)
legal requirements in granting promotional and advertising allowances to
dealers.

BY_____

BUYER _____

TITLE_____
*(To be signed by manufacturers
authorized representative)*

APPROVED_____
Store Advertising Manager

*The NRMA form above is designed as a model agreement useful for various
media or for multi-media promotion. From the samples given, you can develop
an agreement form that satisfies your own needs.*

Proofreaders' marks

Proofreaders, typographers, and your production person all use a standard set of symbols for correcting both manuscript copy and proofs. It's a useful form of shorthand that makes your intentions perfectly clear. Here are the most commonly used symbols and what they mean. (Your paper can provide the whole list of them.)

ℓ	take out	#	space between lines
∧	insert at this point	-/	hyphen
⊙	period	¶	make paragraph
⸝/	comma	no¶	no paragraph
:/	colon	stet	let it stand
;/	semi-colon	tr.	transpose
⸜	apostrophe	caps	capitals
⌐	space between words	l.c.	lower-case letter

How to make changes in copy and proofs

Nobody can guess what you have in mind, so spell it out, using proofreaders' marks and always drawing your corrections out to the margin and circling them so they can be seen and read. This is how you do it.

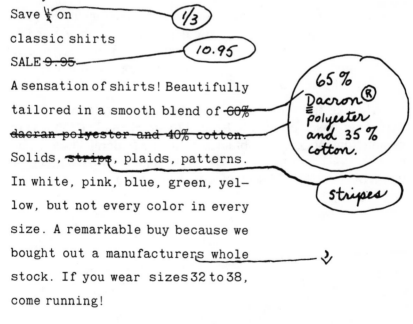

FTC AMENDMENTS OF INTEREST TO

SMALLER STORES

Guides for Advertising Allowances

The Federal Trade Commission amended seven of its "Guides for Advertising Allowances and Other Merchandising Payments and Services" on August 14, 1972. Several of these amendments make it easier for you to get co-op money from your vendors.

1. A manufacturer should not refuse to pay an advertising allowance to retailers who advertise his products at other than manufacturer's suggested prices.

2. A manufacturer should not limit his cooperative advertising program to ads in certain types of newspapers (daily newspapers of general circulation, for example) when other types of papers are commonly used by the smaller customers (like local or weekly papers). However, things like envelope stuffers and handbills are not included in this.

3. A manufacturer may offer to pay all of his customers the same amount for performing a particular service, such as window displays, even though the cost may vary from customer to customer, as long as such payment is in reasonable relationship to the service performed.

If you'd like further information, the NRMA (National Retail Merchants Association) will be glad to supply it. The full text of the amendments can be obtained from the Federal Trade Commission, Washington, D.C. 20580. Ask for Title 16, Commercial Practices, Part 240, Miscellaneous Amendments.

FTC GUIDES AGAINST DECEPTIVE PRICING AND BAIT ADVERTISING

Here is a brief summary of some important FTC rulings. They are not only meant to keep your advertising honest, but to protect you from dishonest and misleading advertising by your competitors. These guides are updated from time to time. For full information, write to the Federal Trade Commission. (If you are a member of the NRMA, the NRMA will keep you posted on changes.)

Former price comparisons

The former price quoted in an ad must be the actual bona fide price at which the article was sold on a regular basis for a reasonably substantial period of time.

If you use comparative language* (regularly, usually, etc.), you must make certain that the comparative is genuine, not fictitious, according to the definition above.

If the word Sale is used, the amount of reduction must not be so insignificant as to be meaningless. For example: when the regular price is $20, you cannot say "Shoe Sale! 19.99".

Comparable value comparisons

When you advertise merchandise, saying that it's at lower price than charged by others in your trading area for the same merchandise, you must be sure that your price is lower than the prevailing price at a substantial number of stores in the area. In other words, you can't say "Shirt Sale 7.50, regular $10 value" if every story in your area, except two tiny boutiques, are also selling the same shirts for 7.50.

Manufacturer's list or suggested retail price

While many customers believe a list or suggested retail price is the one at which something is generally sold, this is not necessarily so. There has been such a widespread failure to observe these prices that only in rare cases are all sales made at these prices. A list price can be legitimately used as a comparative only if it is, indeed, the price regularly charged by retailers in your area. Otherwise its use is misleading.

Bargains based on purchase of other merchandise

This refers to the buy-one-get-one-free or 2-for-1 sale or 1¢ sale, or any sale when additional merchandise is given to the customer if she buys something at a price usually offered by the advertiser. Obviously this is not a "free gift", since a purchase must be made.

All conditions of the offer must be made clear. For example, if the seller increases the price of an item that must be bought, or decreases quantity or quality or attaches other strings to the offer, this must be disclosed.

Miscellaneous price comparisons

1. You must not say "wholesale price" or "factory price" unless these are the prices the customer would pay if the customer bought directly from the manufacturer.

2. You must not offer irregulars or seconds without revealing that the comparative price refers to first quality merchandise.

3. You must not have an "advance" sale when you do not, in good faith, expect to increase the price at a later date.

4. You must not make a "limited" offer which is not, in fact, limited.

In other words: always make sure your bargain offer is genuine and truthful. This is just as good for you as it is for your store's customers.

Bait advertising

This is defined as an alluring but insincere offer to sell something which the advertiser really does not intend or mean to sell. Its purpose is to switch customers to a higher priced item or one that's more advantageous for the advertiser to sell.

1. No ad should include an offer unless it's a bona fide effort to sell the advertised product.

2. No statement or illustrations should be used which create a false impression of grade, quality, make, value, size, color, usability, origin of product, etc., or which may otherwise misrepresent the product in such a manner that later, on disclosure of the actual facts, the purchaser may be switched to another product.

3. The law is violated if the advertiser discourages the purchase of advertised merchandise as part of a bait scheme to sell something else. For example:

   a. refusal to show, demonstrate, or sell the advertised product

   b. disparagement of the advertised product

   c. failure to have enough goods at all outlets listed in the advertisement to meet reasonable demands

   d. refusal to take orders for delivery within a reasonable time

   e. showing of a product which is defective, unusable, or impractical

   f. use of sale plan designed to discourage sales people from selling the advertised merchandise.

4. The advertiser may not make the switch offer after the sale by "unselling" the item through accepting the deposit, then switching to higher priced goods, or through any of the devices listed in 3 above.

*As a general principle, and one that is now being required by the Better Business Bureau of many cities, it is a good idea to watch your comparative language. Terms are not interchangeable.

"Regularly" and "Usually" should be used only when you intend to raise the price again after the sale.

"Formerly", "Originally" and "Reduced" should be used for clearances where the price will not be raised.

"Comparable value", "compares with" and phrases of that sort should be used when you are quoting a price for merchandise you don't usually carry.

"Save" and any of its variations should not be used generally, but limited to a specific sale of specific merchandise.

Care with your comparative language will make your ads more convincing to today's educated and wary consumer. Your Better Business Bureau will be glad to supply additional details, definitions, and such.

GLOSSARY OF ADVERTISING LANGUAGE

We could fill another book with the technical terminology of advertising. Most of which you don't have to know. Most of which your ad reps will be glad to explain to you in detail. However, there are some commonly used terms you should be familiar with, since they are so common. Many are in the text of this book, but we are also including them here for ready reference. And divided them into print, radio, and TV, because each medium speaks its own tongue.

PRINT

AGATE LINE: A space measurement used by newspapers that's one column wide and one-fourteenth of an inch deep.

ART SIZING: The designation of size and type of engraving that's required. This is marked on the drawing because the layout rarely goes to the engraving department with the art.

BENDAY OR BEN DAY: A mechanical process whereby the engraver superimposes gray tones on a line drawing. Benday comes in many tones and textures.

BLOCK OF TYPE: When all lines of type are set flush left and flush right.

CAMERA LUCIDA: An instrument used by artists and designers. For drawing subjects from life, copying drawings or photographs, enlarging or reducing or reversing.

CENTER: Used mostly for display type. All lines of type are centered, leaving various widths to the left and right.

CHARACTER COUNT: The number of type characters that will fit into an area, in a specified style and size of type. It is usually written as 20x6; 20 characters to a line, 6 lines deep.

COLD TYPE: Phototypography. Mostly set by computer on punched tape. The type is then reproduced photographically on film or paper.

COLUMN INCH: A measurement of newspaper space: one column wide, one inch deep.

COMBINATION LINE AND HALF-TONE: All line and black areas kept solid, rest of the art translated into tones of gray.

COMBINATION LINE AND HALF-TONE — DROP WHITES: As above, but with all white areas in the drawing dropped out, either photographically or manually.

COMP (COMPREHENSIVE): A hand-made facsimile of an ad showing the way it will appear in the newspaper.

COPY COUNT: The number of type characters that will fit into an area of the layout, based on the relationship of the size of typewriter type to the type requested.

CRAFTINT: The trade name of a product that lets the artist put a screened dot on a line drawing. This simulates a half-tone or Benday screen. In many dots and textures.

CROMOLITE: One of several trade-mark products, it's a chemical used by artists to replace water in a "wash" drawing. The art is then sprayed with another chemical by the engraver and filtered through the camera lens so the reproduction of half-tone engravings is improved.

DEMOGRAPHICS: Characteristics of audience (for any medium) by age, sex, occupation, education, economic status, etc.

DEPTH OF COLUMN: The agate line or inch measurement of a column from top to bottom.

DISPLAY TYPE: Often called headline or sub-headline type. From 16 point up.

FIXED LOCATION: The same position in the newspaper, in every issue.

FLUSH LEFT: All lines of type are aligned on the left side. Type lines are random width on the right.

FLUSH RIGHT: As above, but lines are aligned on the right side.

GUTTER: The blank space on the inside margins of the newspaper.

HALF-TONE: A reproduction process that translates the gray tones in drawings and photographs into dots.

HOT TYPE: Typography that is set from pre-cast type letter by letter or machine-set by casting letters, words, or lines from hot metal.

LAYOUT MARK-UP: The information on the layout for the mechanical completion of an ad. This includes such details as type name and size, key letters, copy, art, logotype, borders, etc.

LEADING: The space between lines of type. ''Set Solid'' is as tight as the lines can be set.

LINAGE: The number of agate lines of one or more ads in the newspaper.

LINE: One-fourteenth of an inch.

LINE CUT: An engraving made from art or type when the line or area is solid black.

LINE-FOR-LINE: Copy is set exactly as it is typed, each line of type ending where the line of typed copy ends.

MAKE-UP: The arrangement of printed material on a page or in an issue of the paper.

MECHANICAL: Camera-ready copy. Every element of the ad is pasted into position, ready for the engraver in one unit.

MILLINE RATE: The cost of one line of advertising per million circulation at the lowest line rate, minus space and frequency discounts.

OFFSET PRINTING: A process in which the impression is transferred from the engraving plate to a rubber blanket and then printed on paper.

POINT: There are 72 points to the inch. The point size indicates the height of the type letter.

PREFERRED POSITION: An especially desirable position in the paper. Often obtained by paying an extra charge; sometimes given to a heavy advertiser.

REVERSE TYPE: White type on a black or gray area, either background or art.

ROP: Run-of-paper position; anywhere in the newspaper. ROP color is a color ad placed anywhere in the regular sections of the paper.

SILHOUETTE HALF-TONE: Half-tone dots covering an irregular shape that follows the silhouette of the artwork.

SQUARE HALF-TONE: Despite its name, the engraving can be any shape: square, oblong, round. The half-tone dot covers the entire area.

SURPRINT TYPE: Black type superimposed over art or a gray area.

VELOX PRINT: Photographic reproduction of original art in a specified size. It can be all line, all half-tone, or a combination of line and half-tone.

WAIT ORDER: Sometimes also called Display Order. An ad that is set in type, held for further instruction. Proof is sent to store.

RADIO

ANNOUNCEMENT: Commercial or spot. Message of 60, 30, or 10 seconds.

AVAILABILITIES: Time slots where commercials can be placed. Often shortened to "avails".

BTA: Run of schedule: station schedules spots at Best Time Available. If better times become available, spots are upgraded.

COMBINATION RATE: Reduced rates from two or more stations, such as sister AM and FM stations, or stations with a geographical tie-in.

COST PER THOUSAND: The cost for radio time to reach 1000 listeners.

CUMULATIVE AUDIENCE: Also called "cume". Audience reached by a station over an extended period of time, during part of the day, the whole day, or a week.

DRIVE TIME: The morning and afternoon. AM drive time is usually 6 to 10 a.m. PM drive time usually 4 to 7 p.m. Also called Traffic or Commuter time.

EVENING: Radio time slot that usually runs from 7 p.m. to midnight.

FIXED POSITION: Spot will be delivered at a guaranteed time, say 6:29 p.m. every day. An extra charge for this guarantee.

FLIGHT: A specific and intensive campaign, usually on a single event or idea within a relatively limited time.

FREQUENCY: Average number of times an advertiser's message reaches an individual in a specified period of time.

HOUSEWIFE TIME: Usually between 10 a.m. and 3 p.m.

ID: Short for identification. A 10-second commercial.

LIVE COPY: Copy read by announcer, in contrast to taped messages.

NIGHT TIME: Time slot from midnight to 6 a.m.

OPEN-END: Taped commercial that leaves room at the end for "live" tag.

PREMIUM RATE: Extra charge for special valuable time: fixed position, news, special events, weather, etc.

REACH: The number of different individuals a program or commercial reaches in a given time period or combination of time periods.

REMOTE: A broadcast from some place other than the station's studio.

SATURATION: A heavy schedule of spots to reach as many listeners as possible as quickly as possible.

SEPARATION: The station provides a set time period between commercials by competitors.

SHARE OF AUDIENCE: Percentage of tuned-in audience listening to each station at any given time.

STRIP: Program or spot bought at the same time each day.

TENS: 10-second commercials.

THIRTIES: 30-second commercials.

VERTICAL SATURATION: Slotting commercials heavily on several stations for a limited time to reach maximum number of listeners.

TELEVISION

ACROSS-THE-BOARD: Spots scheduled at the same time from Monday through Friday or Monday through Sunday. A "board" is a week.

ANIMATION: Action imparted to still artwork by shooting it frame by frame.

ANSWER PRINT: First composite film print struck from negative. Equivalent to a proof. First acceptable answer print then becomes the release print.

AVERAGE AUDIENCE: Also called AA. Percentage of TV households tuned in to a program during an average minute.

BLEED: Amount allowable around the picture that can be lost by the home set without spoiling message.

CPM: Cost per thousand. Cost to reach 1000 homes or people.

CLOSE-UP: A very close camera shot to show detail. Also called tight shot.

CRAWL: Words or artwork that moves up or down or side to side across the TV screen.

DAY PARTS: Times of telecast. Usually divided into morning, afternoon, early evening, night, and late night.

DISSOLVE: A fade-out of pictures or words while other pictures or words appear. Can be slow or fast.

ECU: Extreme close-up, generally a head-shot.

FIXED RATE: Price for time slot which guarantees that the commercial will run at that time and not be pre-empted.

FREQUENCY: Average number of times an unduplicated audience viewed a TV schedule.

GROSS RATING POINTS: Also called GRP's. The sum of the audiences for each commercial in a schedule.

HORIZONTAL SATURATION: Intensive schedule of spots at the same time for several days to target an audience that views at that time.

ID: Station identification; also 10-second spot.

KINE: (Pronounced "kinny"). Short for kinescope; filming of TV program from a monitor.

LS: Long shot.

PIGGYBACK: A long commercial, made up of two short individual commercials for different items, placed back to back.

PRE-EMPTIBLE SPOTS: Commercials sold at reduced rates with the station having the option of selling same time to advertiser who will pay full rates.

PRIME TIME: Hours between 7:30 p.m. to 11 p.m. in Eastern, Mountain and Pacific time zones; 6:30 to 10 p.m. in Central time zone.

ROS: Run of station. Commercials bought to run at station's discretion at any time.

REACH: Number or percent of audience exposed to one or more messages.

SATURATION: Heavy use of commercials in a short period of time.

SHARE OF AUDIENCE: The percentage of total TV viewing audience tuned to a program in a given time period.

SPLIT SCREEN: TV screen electronically divided to show two or more pictures at once.

STORYBOARD: Artwork showing the sequence of a TV commercial, including all major visual changes.

SYNC: Matching of sound to picture.

UNDUPLICATED AUDIENCE: Number of viewers reached at least once by a TV schedule.

VOICE OVER: When speaker's voice is broadcast but speaker is not shown.

Many of the definitions above are based on booklets issued by The Newspaper Advertising Bureau, Inc., the Radio Advertising Bureau, Inc., and the Television Bureau of Advertising, Inc. All of whom we thank for their help in compiling this glossary.

INDEX

A

B

C

186

187

F

G

H

I

191

ABOUT THE AUTHORS

Judy Young Ocko is probably the only copywriter in the country with a Ph.D. in Archaeology. Her first writing job was with Bernice Fitzgibbon at Gimbels, New York. From there she went to Bamberger's, then to an advertising agency. This was followed by Divisional Ad Manager at Macy's, then Copy Chief for Gimbels. Since that time she has free-lanced. Mrs. Ocko's clients include everything from specialty stores to a meat packer to ad agencies. She teaches at the Tobe-Coburn School for Fashion Careers in New York and lectures extensively. In 1974, she was elected to the Retail Advertising Hall of Fame. She and her husband live in New York City and have a weekend house in New Jersey.

Morris L. Rosenblum, known wherever retail ads are created as "Rosy", is a graduate of Pratt Institute who made him its Alumnus of the Year in 1969. From Art Director of Abraham and Straus, he went on to be Art and Display Director of Bamberger's. Then, after 3 years as president of an advertising agency, he joined Macy's New York where he became Vice President and Creative Director in 1965. He added Emeritus to this title in 1973. He is now a consultant to large and small stores across the country. His many, many awards include the NRMA silver medal award for his contributions to the retail industry and election to the Retail Hall of Fame. In 1972 he was Chairman of the Sales Promotion Division of the NRMA. He and his wife live in Lake Worth, Florida.

BOOKS ON ADVERTISING

Ocko, J.Y. "Retail Advertising Copy: The How, The What, The Why".

Rosenblum, M.L. "How to Design Effective Store Advertising"

Ocko & Rosenblum "The Secret Ingredient of Good Retail Ads: a Handbook for Buyers and their Bosses".

(all available from the National Retail Merchants Association, 100 W. 31 St., New York, N.Y. 10001)

NOTES

NOTES